Needlepoint
Techniques and Projects

By the Editors of Sunset Books
and Sunset Magazine

Lane Publishing Co. • Menlo Park, California

Pretty, Popular, and Practical

The three "P's" mentioned above apply not only to needlepoint as a craft, but to the book you hold in your hands as well. For your enjoyment, and for visual ease, we've included full-color photographs of *all* projects, as well as color graphs and finishing art. Pages 6 to 31 stress the basics, and they have been edited to provide ready reference not only for beginners but for more experienced needlepointers who may wish to refresh their memories on a certain technique. Add to this an array of delightfully varied project ideas — ranging from pincushions and pictures to pillows and purses — and you have not only a beautiful, but a beautifully practical, book that's sure to bring hours of stitching pleasure to all needlepoint devotees.

We would like to extend our sincere appreciation to the following individuals whose considerable efforts and talents have combined to produce so much of this book: for hours and hours of nimble-fingered stitching, many thanks to Carroll Bozarth (Hopi Indian Clutch), Linda Carss (Strawberry Basket pillow), Erma Paulson (Cereal Box pillow), and Lucy St. John (Parrot Parade pillow, Hopi Indian Eyeglass Case, 1903 Sunset Cover, and all stitch samples). All other projects were skillfully stitched by the designers themselves.

Special thanks go to Sandy Novack and Randi Sandy of Designcrafts of California, for their advice and technical expertise in finishing all of the projects (with the exception of framing done for "1903 Sunset Cover" and "Victorian House" projects) featured in this book.

Supervising Editor:
Alyson Smith Gonsalves

Research and Text:
Diane Petrica Tapscott

Design: Tonya Carpenter
Illustrations: Marsha Cooke

Photography: All photographs in this book are by Jerry Wainwright except as follows: Ells Marugg, 7 all, 8 all, 12 lower right, 16 all, 21 all except upper right, 22 upper right, 25 upper right, and 27 center and lower right.

Cover: Strawberry Basket pillow (page 72) designed by Sue Walther. Photographed by Norman A. Plate.

Sunset Books
  Editor, David E. Clark
  Managing Editor, Elizabeth L. Hogan

Sixth printing August 1987

Contents

Needlepoint: Yesterday and Today

Needlepoint's resurgence as a favored handcraft is one more reminder that history repeats itself. The gradual development of needlepoint over the centuries into the yarn and canvas craft with which we are familiar has come about through a number of historical ups and downs.

An Illustrious Past

Necessity being the mother of invention, needlepoint had its beginnings many centuries ago when the ancient Egyptians, originally a nation of tent dwellers, devised a sturdy stitch with which to secure the flaps of their tents. This stitch — a merely functional use of needle and thread for the Egyptians — eventually became the tent stitch, the basic stitch of needlepoint.

But it wasn't until the 15th century that needlepoint emerged as a popular handcraft for decorative as well as functional purposes. In the 16th century, with the introduction of steel embroidery needles, interest in "canvas embroidery" (as it is called in Europe) began to grow, attracting wealthy — even royal — patrons. Henry VIII of England was a great patron of heraldic embroidery, a fact that quite possibly inspired his daughter Elizabeth to while away many tedious hours in the Tower of London stitching needlepoint.

Not until the Victorian era did needlepoint really become fashionable in the United States. The development of aniline dyes in the 19th century helped to advance this popularity by providing a vast array of bright, chemically colored yarns for needlework. The innovation of machine-made embroidery canvas also contributed to this rise in popularity by providing an inexpensive, uniform ground on which to work these exciting new yarns.

During most of the 19th century, women were feverishly stitching upholstery, fire screens, slippers, pill boxes, purses, billfolds, and vests — in other words, just about anything and everything was needlepointed.

But as the technological age pushed humanity into the 20th century, life styles altered immensely, particularly in

FINE DETAIL and meticulous stitching of yesterday are illustrated by 18th century American needlework (top) and 16th century European canvas embroidery (above). Photograph details courtesy Museum of Fine Arts, Boston.

America. Where women had once been confined both physically and socially in their homes, they now began to gradually experience a taste of freedom. With the coming of World War I, women found themselves actually working in factories to supplement the job force. This increased involvement brought the gradual realization: why spend hours stitching when fabric could be so easily and inexpensively purchased? And so handcrafts such as needlepoint were gradually relegated to Grandma's work basket.

Trends Today

By the 1960s, though, the values and inclinations of the older generation came to be questioned by a younger generation disenchanted with the monotony and stamped-out patterns of a technological life style. Young people felt a strong need to return to the simple pleasures of life, with the result that many crafts have been enthusiastically revived — and needlepoint, for one, is basking in the popularity it so richly deserves.

Because it's an easy-to-learn, rather inexpensive retreat from the wear and tear of our fast-paced lives, needlepoint has found enthusiastic support among men as well as among women. And the input of a number of talented, adventuresome designers constantly provides the stitcher with a cornucopia of new needlepoint designs.

Even those of you who find sewing on a button a frustrating experience can take part in this revival. We show you how to do the basic needlepoint stitches, a number of decorative stitches, and a sampling of bargello patterns. Pages 32–79 include complete, easy-to-understand instructions for a variety of interesting projects and all related finishing techniques. And if you're feeling adventurous, try designing your own; we've included everything you'll need.

Needlepoint is a versatile craft — you can learn the fundamentals in an hour; after that it can be as leisurely or as challenging as you wish. This book is designed to inspire and guide you into the special world of yarn and canvas.

TODAY, people of all persuasions are enjoying needlepoint—and why not? Anyone can learn the basics in a very short time; from then on, it's just plain fun.

Materials at a Minimum

You needn't invest a nest egg in costly tools and equipment to get started in needlepoint; that's part of the beauty of it. With only a few basic materials — canvas, yarn, and needles — you can learn the stitches and techniques of this alluring art. Read this section carefully to acquaint yourself with needlepoint materials at a minimum.

A Foundation to Grow On - Canvas

Just as canvas is the foundation for a painting, so it is for needlepoint — a painter's canvas holding and containing the pigments that adorn it, the needleworker's canvas providing the base for all needlepoint stitches. Yet the stitcher's canvas is quite different from that of a painter. Needlepoint canvas is more loosely constructed and has the appearance of screening used for windows.

Usually made of cotton or polyester — sometimes of linen — needlepoint canvas is coated with sizing to give it body and strength. It is bleached to white or left in its natural ecru color, and is available in widths ranging from 24 to 56 inches.

The canvas you select will influence the final appearance of your needlepoint project; read further to see why.

Mono, Leno, or Penelope?

These are the names given to the three structural types of needlepoint canvas. The intersection of threads, called the "mesh," distinguishes one canvas from another. Refer to the photos below as you read their descriptions.

• Mono canvas consists of single threads evenly woven in vertical (warp) and horizontal (woof) directions.

• Leno canvas resembles mono canvas. Though it appears to be single-threaded, it actually consists of two warp threads (both running in the same direction, parallel to the selvage) twisted together to hold a third thread, running in the woof direction (perpendicular to the warp), in a more stable position. Leno canvas can be stitched with the double threads running either vertically or horizontally.

• Penelope canvas, or double-threaded canvas, has four threads at each mesh: two threads woven closely in the warp direction and two threads spaced slightly apart in the woof direction. The warp threads (closely woven) run in the same direction as the selvage, and penelope canvas should be worked with the warp threads running from the top to the bottom of your design.

Leno canvas is sometimes chosen over mono because during stitching, leno threads hold firm and mono threads tend to shift. But for the beginner, mono or leno is usually the choice over penelope. Mono and leno are somewhat easier to work with than penelope, for your eyes adjust more readily to their open mesh.

Penelope's four-thread mesh is nevertheless more versatile than either mono or leno. You can work penelope canvas as if it were a single-threaded canvas, covering the entire four-thread mesh with one stitch. Or you can separate the warp threads slightly with a needle, giving more meshes over which to stitch—and by using each of these smaller meshes individually, you can incorporate small areas of fine petit point detail within larger background areas (see page 8). To determine which canvas you prefer, try all three types as you practice the stitches.

Another canvas, called bargello canvas, is actually a mono or leno canvas with qualities that make it useful for bargello pattern work (see page 26). Because the threads of bargello canvas are more fibrous than those of other canvases, stitches are prevented from slipping, and the result is better coverage of the canvas. Heavily sized to hold its shape, bargello canvas is a darker color than most canvases; this helps prevent its showing through after the surface has been stitched.

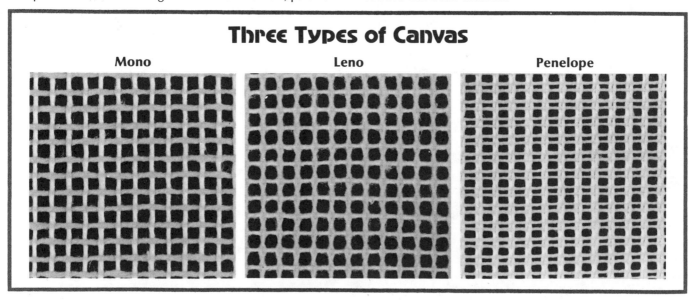

Three Types of Canvas

| Mono | Leno | Penelope |

Coordinating Canvas, Yarns, and Needles

#18 canvas
1 strand Persian
#22 needle

#16 canvas
1 strand Persian
#20 needle

#14 canvas
2 strands Persian
#19–20 needle

#10 canvas
3 strands Persian
#18 needle

#7 canvas
4–6 strands Persian
#16–18 needle

#5 canvas
7–9 strands Persian
#13–14 needle

Consider the Gauge of Canvas

The number of threads per inch determines the gauge of canvas. For example, #10 mono or leno canvas has 10 threads per inch running horizontally and 10 threads per inch running vertically. One square inch of #10 canvas will therefore hold 100 stitches. Penelope canvas is designated differently — #10 penelope is described by the figure 10/20, indicating that 10 stitches can be worked over one row of horizontal or vertical double meshes in 1 inch, or 20 stitches can be worked in the same row in 1 inch if you separate the warp threads.

The smaller the gauge, the more stitches per inch and the more time required for the completion of the same canvas area. For instance, 1 square inch of #18 canvas holds 324 stitches; covering this will take more than three times as long as covering a square inch of #10 canvas (see below). As you can see, the hours you spend stitching are greatly affected by the gauge of canvas you select.

Petit point, gros point, and quick point are terms used to express a range of gauges. Quick point refers to canvas gauges #3 to #7; gros point to gauges #8 to #14; and petit point to gauges #18 to #40. Generally, quick point canvases are used for making rugs or very large items, so you may see it called "rug canvas," though gros point canvas may also be used for rugs.

Canvas Queries

Now that you have a fair idea of what canvas is, you're a step closer to going shopping. But what color is best? Is width important? Is one canvas better than another? Such questions will probably arise when you're faced with several rolls of canvas.

Width. Canvas comes in widths of 24, 36, and 40 inches; rug canvas sometimes can be found in 56-inch width. The larger the mesh, the wider the canvas. Finer mesh petit point canvas is usually 24 inches wide.

Buy the width of canvas that best suits your needs; don't try to scrimp. Better to allow for extra canvas, for it's very disappointing to find that the pillow you spent hours on is going to be swallowed by your sofa because it's too small. Unless you're making a very large piece, you'll probably have canvas left over, but it can always be used for other projects.

Color. Whether you choose white canvas or ecru will depend on your proposed design. White canvas suits predominantly light-colored designs; ecru is better for darker designs.

Occasionally stitches of unequal tension will shift or pull away from neighboring stitches, allowing the canvas to peek through. For this reason, the color of the yarn and the color of the canvas should be as compatible as possible to prevent exposed canvas from marring the overall effect of your design.

If you are working with a handpainted or screen-printed canvas on which yarn colors have been indicated with paints or pigments, the color of your canvas will not noticeably affect your design.

Quality. Suppose you're looking for 10/20 penelope canvas and a store has two rolls to choose from: one is $6 a yard and the other is $8. Why pay $8 when you could pay $6? If you look closely at the canvas, you might find differences other than price — the less expensive canvas may have defects you'll notice only in a careful examination. On the other hand, the less expensive canvas may have been manufactured by a larger company that can afford to sell for less because it sells in greater volume.

As with anything you purchase, quality items usually cost more, but not always. You want the highest quality canvas for the best price — and the surest means to that end is careful inspection of the canvas.

Watch for such defects as knotted, joined, thin, or weak threads. During the blocking process, canvas undergoes great strain, and such flaws can snap, ruining your work.

Canvas should appear to be polished; this indicates that it has been coated wtih sizing to keep it from becoming limp or misshapen as you stitch. Don't be alarmed to find the larger mesh canvases (#3 through #8) stiffer than others; because of the large mesh, more sizing is needed to hold the shape of the canvas.

Finally, check to be certain that the canvas has evenly woven squares. Unevenness is a defect you probably won't see too often, but if you work on such canvas it will cause unsightly stitching.

Working Petit Point

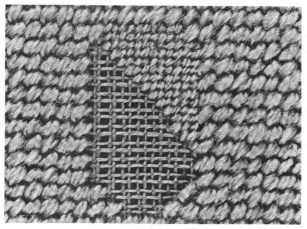

TO WORK petit point on 10/20 penelope canvas, separate the double vertical threads with your needle tip; then stitch over added meshes.

Comparing Canvas Gauge

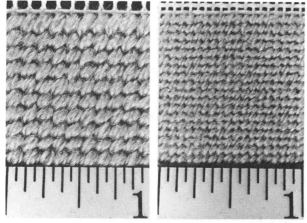

WHILE 1 square inch of #10 canvas yields 100 stitches (left), 1 square inch of #18 canvas yields 324 (right).

Yarns-Color With Character

If you're at all hesitant about learning needlepoint, just walk into a needlepoint shop or the art needlework department of a large store and feast your eyes on the rich display of dazzling yarns. No doubt your fingers will begin to itch with the anticipation of stitching your first needlepoint project. But before you wreak havoc on your pocketbook, read further to learn what you should look for when purchasing needlepoint yarns.

The most important quality needlepoint yarn must have is to be made of long, smooth fibers that remain strong during constant pulling through the canvas. Yarn of this quality will not weaken or break while being worked.

Naturals for Needlepoint

Though there are times when synthetic yarns can be used for needlepoint, yarns made of natural fibers (wool, cotton, and linen) have qualities of luster and durability that can't be matched by synthetics. Also, most natural yarns today are colorfast and mothproof.

Persian yarn is three-ply yarn consisting of three strands loosely twisted together. Originally developed for the repair of Persian carpets, this yarn is long-wearing and comes in more than 400 colors.

Persian wool may be more expensive than other needlepoint yarns, but it is certainly the most versatile. The strands are easily separated to be used on canvases of various gauges, and they can be plied together to produce even more subtle color variations.

Persian yarn is sold in varying quantities, from as little as a single thread (about 33 inches) to 8-ounce skeins of approximately 320 yards each. At one time Persian yarn might have been difficult to obtain, but needlepoint's popularity has encouraged the availability of these yarns.

Tapestry wool, a 4-ply, tightly twisted yarn, is less expensive than Persian yarn, but it is dyed in fewer colors. Tapestry yarn can be separated into single strands and is generally sold in 40-yard skeins.

Embroidery-type threads such as crewel wool, perle cotton, and embroidery silk or floss can all be used for needlepoint. One thread of crewel wool — much finer than Persian or tapestry wool — is ideal for petit point.

A 2-ply thread with a distinctive luster, perle cotton may add just the right accent to your piece.

Six-ply cotton embroidery floss is more difficult to work with than perle cotton, as individual strands can be pulled out of place while you stitch. Mercerized for strength and shine, embroidery floss does have a character of its own. Both cotton embroidery floss and perle cotton are found in a wide range of colors.

Embroidery silk, also 6-ply, is the most expensive material for needlepoint, yard for yard. Used to highlight small areas, it can be lovely, but it is slippery and temperamental to work with. Even the slightest rough patch of skin on your hand could cause a snag. Experienced needlepointers often run embroidery silk over a piece of beeswax to make their work easier.

Rug yarn is a thicker, rougher, 3-ply yarn used primarily on canvas sizes #8 and lower, though you can experiment with rug yarn on finer mesh canvas for different effects. Rya rug yarn, a tightly twisted Scandinavian woolen rug yarn, is considered to be the best.

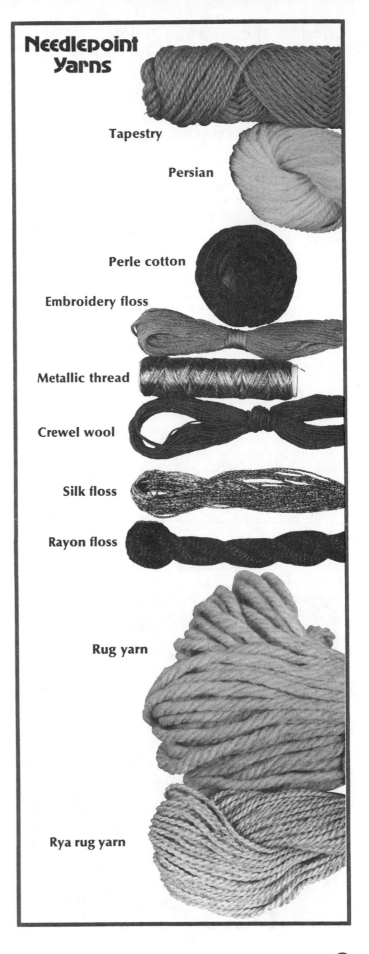

Needlepoint Yarns

Tapestry

Persian

Perle cotton

Embroidery floss

Metallic thread

Crewel wool

Silk floss

Rayon floss

Rug yarn

Rya rug yarn

Consider These—with Caution

There are some needlepointers who would gasp at the thought of using anything but pure wool yarns for needlepoint. But the yarn industry is constantly trying to produce better imitations of the natural fibers; you might like to experiment with some for unusual effects.

Rayon embroidery floss, for example, can give a sheen to accent small areas of a design. For larger areas, be careful. Synthetic yarns — orlon, rayon, and acrylic, for instance — tend to pill and don't last as long as the natural fibers. Rayon is far less expensive than silk. It can be mixed with strands of natural fibers.

Knitting worsted and other yarns made from short fibers (natural or synthetic) should be avoided. Short-fibered yarns fluff up, break easily, and are too elastic, making them difficult to work with for needlepoint. These are best left for knitters and crocheters.

With these thoughts in mind, go ahead and experiment with many yarns. If you like the effect a certain yarn gives, and it handles well, by all means use it. Record your discoveries — a list of characteristics such as cost, color range, size of skeins, availability, and the amount of yarn it takes to stitch 1 square inch will be an invaluable source to have, particularly if you would like to design your own needlepoint projects.

Yarn Count

How much yarn is enough to stitch a certain area? The most accurate method for determining the amount of yarn to buy for needlepoint is to follow this basic formula:

1. Select the type of yarn you will use, keeping in mind the number of strands required to cover one mesh of the canvas you have chosen (see chart on page 7).
2. Cut some measured lengths of a yarn similar to that which you have chosen and stitch a 1-inch square in the stitch you plan to use.
3. Approximate the number of square inches in each color area of your design.
4. Multiply the number of square inches in each color by the length of yarn used to stitch 1 square inch. The total of these calculations will give you the approximate amount of yarn (in yards) to purchase for each color of yarn you select.

Remember: When using only a part of a thread of yarn — one strand of Persian yarn for #18 canvas, for example — you'll need less yarn. On the other hand, if you're using more than a full thread — such as 9 strands for #3 canvas — you'll need more yarn.

Make allowances. Few things are more distressing than to run out of yarn before finishing a project. To allow for errors, tension changes, and starting and ending threads, purchase a few extra yards of yarn beyond the amount you've calculated. Excess yarn can always be used for another project, for practicing decorative stitches, or just to keep as a color reference.

Most yarn suppliers will give you credit for any unbroken skeins you wish to return. It's best to ask a shopkeeper, before you buy the yarn, if this is the policy of the store (in most cases it is).

Dye lots. If you wait to complete your purchase of any single yarn color, you may have difficulty buying yarn of the same shade, as yarn colors vary slightly from dye lot to dye lot. A dye lot is a batch of yarn which has been dyed at the same time in the same dye bath.

Dye baths vary for a variety of reasons, producing slight changes in shade that could be enough to mar the appearance of your piece. For this reason, you should buy all the yarn needed for a large area at one time. You needn't purchase each individual yarn color for smaller areas all at once, just all you need of one color. Sometimes a shopkeeper will set aside yarn of a dye lot for possible future purchase; check to see if this is feasible.

If you have difficulty estimating the exact amount of yarn for your project, take your design and canvas with you when you go to buy yarn. Usually needlepoint shops have experienced staff members who can, by sight, estimate the amount of yarn you will need.

Needles Are Your Number One Tools

Needlepoint needles are generally sold in packages of six and are called tapestry needles. They vary in size from #13, the largest, to #24, the smallest.

A tapestry needle has a large eye made especially smooth for easy threading, preventing unnecessary fraying of yarns. The point of the needle is blunt so that it will not split the canvas threads or catch previously worked stitches.

A "strawberry emery" attached to an inexpensive pincushion is a helpful item. Periodically push the point of your needle into the emery. This will clean the needle and keep it from dragging between the meshes of your canvas.

Having read about canvas, yarn, and needles, refer to the chart on page 7; it is a guide for coordinating these materials, all of which must work well together to produce beautiful needlepoint.

Needles to Use

Curved upholsterer's needle

Needle threader   #22

#20

#18

embroidery scissors

14

And Then There Are Extras

Canvas, yarn, and needles are the needlepointer's basic tools, but there are a few more supplies you might consider having on hand. You probably already have some of these:

- Small, sharp scissors for snipping yarn.
- Large scissors for cutting canvas.
- Pincushion with a strawberry emery.
- Thimble to protect your finger. If you are not accustomed to wearing a thimble and find it awkward, try wrapping an adhesive bandage around your finger.
- Masking tape or cloth tape, 1 inch wide, for binding edges of canvas.
- Ruler, preferably 18 inches long; a yardstick and measuring tape are useful, too.
- Needle threader (see page 10).
- Indelible markers for drawing on canvas. Test all markers for indelibility by drawing on a piece of scrap canvas; then wet and dry the canvas to see if the ink has run. We recommend a gray marker.
- Acrylic and/or oil paints, to paint on canvas.
- Paintbrushes (oil and watercolor) in a variety of sizes.
- Graph and tracing paper for working the initial design.
- Frame to prevent canvas from being pulled out of shape during stitching. Though frames make the work less portable, some needlepointers prefer them. Experiment with four inexpensive stretcher bars, the kind found in art supply stores.
- Blocking materials (see page 29).
- Finishing materials (see individual projects).

A final word — a finished needlepoint project will last only as long as the materials from which it is made. This could be 100 years or more — so quality counts.

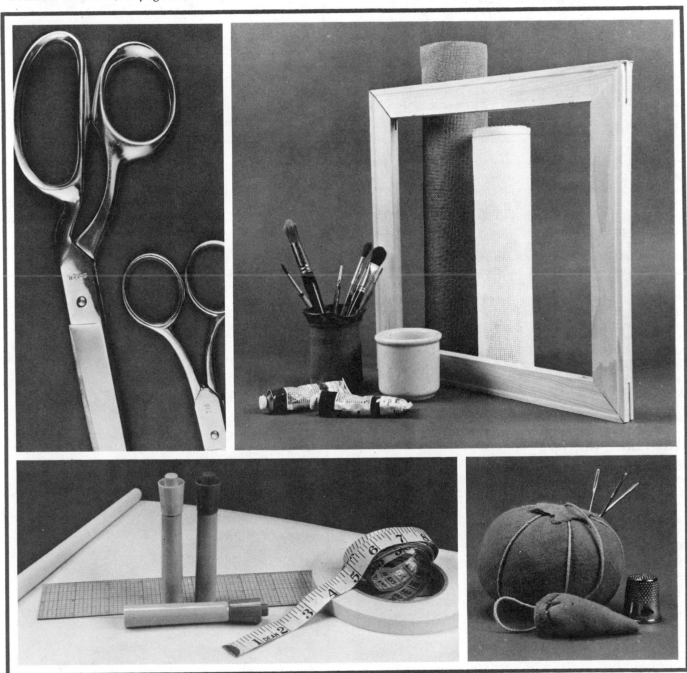

Needlepoint Techniques

Needlepoint can be a simple and leisurely craft. Materials are easy to find, stitches are fun to learn, and most projects are pleasantly portable. To get started, you'll want to read the basic guidelines that follow and return to them whenever you have questions or need a review.

Enlarging and Reducing Your Design

Suppose you select just the right design to reproduce in needlepoint, but it's larger or smaller than the piece you want to make? The problem of altering the size of a design has some easy solutions. For enlarging the designs in this book, use either of the following methods. The grid method, though, is the most economical and is a valuable technique to learn.

The Grid Method

This is an easy and inexpensive method for enlarging or reducing designs. First trace the original design onto a piece of paper that has been marked in a grid pattern of identical squares. These can measure anywhere from ¼ to 1 inch, depending on the size of the design. Smaller designs should have smaller squares; larger designs, larger squares.

On another piece of paper, draw a second grid pattern — smaller or larger, depending upon whether you are reducing or enlarging the designs—with all squares equal to a definite percentage size of the original grid squares. Copy the design from each block of the first grid onto the corresponding block of the second grid. Remember that your second grid must have exactly the same number of squares as the first grid. If, for example, you have an 8-inch design and want to use it for a 16-inch pillow, draw a 1-inch grid over the 8-inch tracing and a second grid 100 percent larger, leaving 2-inch squares. By transferring the corresponding blocks, you'll have accurately doubled the size of the first design (see fig. 12-A).

The Photo Copy

Probably the simplest, though most costly, method for enlarging or reducing a design is to take it to a professional photo copier. Look under Photo Copying or Blue Printers in the Yellow Pages of your phone book for a photo copier near you. If the design is a black and white picture with gray tones, or a color picture, ask for a positive print (see fig. 12-B). Because prices for this service vary, you'll be wise to call first to get an estimate. For instance, the enlargement of a 6-inch square into a 16-inch square can cost about $8.

For about half the cost of a positive print, you can order a line stat (see fig. 12-B). First make an accurate tracing of your design in a fine line pen, drawing only the main outlines. Then give the tracing to the photo copier and ask for a line stat enlarged or reduced to the scale you need. You can save money with a line stat if indications of

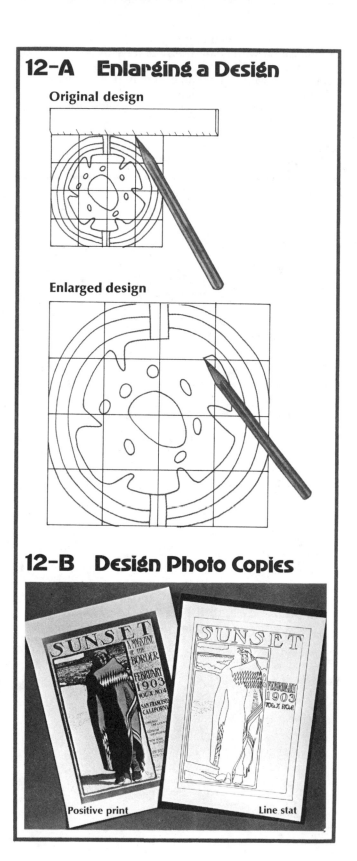

12-A Enlarging a Design

Original design

Enlarged design

12-B Design Photo Copies

Positive print   Line stat

shading and gray areas aren't necessary to the understanding of your design.

Preparing the Canvas

Choosing a design and gathering the necessary materials will probably put you in the mood to begin stitching immediately. But several things must be done first — as you read on, study figure 13-A.

1. Cut your canvas the size of your working area plus 2 to 3 inches on all sides (as a margin). For example, a 15-inch square pillow requires at least a 19-inch square of canvas.

2. Bind all edges with masking tape — 1-inch tape is sufficient. This smooth binding prevents canvas threads from raveling and also keeps the yarn from snagging on the edge of the canvas while you work.

3. Mark one edge of the canvas as the TOP to remind yourself not to stitch in the wrong direction.

4. Fold the canvas into quarters.

5. Mark a "+" in the center.

6. Count out both horizontally and vertically along the meshes to establish the design's border, and use an indelible marker to outline the design area. For instance, a 15-inch square pillow done on #10 mono canvas would cover 150 meshes (75 meshes on each side of the center).

7. Mark the center point of each edge of the canvas.

8. On a piece of brown paper, draw the outline of the canvas and mark the center points of the edges. This will be your guide when you block your piece—the canvas will be pulled and stretched to match this outline. (See Blocking, page 29.)

From Concept to Canvas

If you speak to a number of experienced needleworkers, you'll hear of at least three methods of getting from sketch to stitch. The first method, graphing a design, involves the use of a grid pattern of small squares in which each square represents one intersection of canvas threads, or one diagonal stitch. This grid pattern, called a needlepoint graph or chart, is usually worked out on graph paper measured off into squares (or stitches) per inch (see project graphs, pages 34 to 79). The needlepoint design is transferred onto this grid, square for square, so that actual stitches can be counted out as you work — a tedious method, yet the most accurate if you wish to exactly reproduce a design.

The second method is to trace the outlines of your design directly onto the canvas and then use your sketched design as a color reference from which to work the needlepoint stitches. This method is less precise than the grid pattern approach just described, but for most designs it is adequate.

The third method, thought by some to be the easiest, is to paint the design in full colors onto the canvas and then stitch accordingly.

Detailed descriptions of all three methods follow.

Graphing a design. Begin by lightly tracing your design (in the actual size) with pencil onto graph paper that corresponds to the gauge of canvas you intend to use. For example, 10-squares-to-the-inch graph paper is just right for #10 canvas. You'll find that most graph paper is 10 to the inch or larger (8 or 6 squares to the inch), but that's not a problem — a needlepoint chart for #12 or #14 can-

13-A Preparing a Canvas

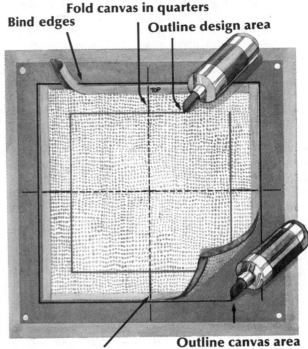

Bind edges
Fold canvas in quarters
Outline design area
Outline canvas area
Mark centers of sides on canvas and on brown paper

13-B Graphing a Design

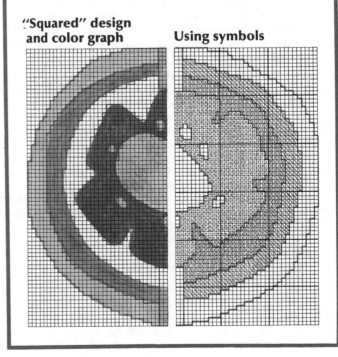

"Squared" design and color graph

Using symbols

vas can be worked on 10-to-the-inch graph paper even though it will be slightly larger than your finished stitched piece. Draw darker lines every 12 or 14 lines to help keep your place.

After tracing the design onto graph paper, "square" the outlines of each color area in the design to conform to the squares of the grid (see fig. 13-B). This will take time, depending upon the intricacy of your design, but it is an excellent learning technique for the beginner. Making a needlepoint graph gives you a better understanding of how to interpret designs into a grid formation on canvas.

After drawing in the color area outlines on the graph, you can color in the chart with colored pencils, crayons, felt markers, or watercolor paints to indicate the colors of yarn you intend to use; this graph should be treated as a guide, not as a duplicate of the finished piece.

If you don't have a coloring medium and would rather not buy any, you can indicate color by the use of symbols. For instance, mark an "X" for blue, a dot for green, a diagonal line for yellow, and so on, in each square of the grid where that color will appear. Though using symbols is an adequate method, a colored graph is a much easier reference to follow, for the eye can distinguish colors more readily than symbols (see fig. 13-B).

Having completed the graph, you can begin to work directly from it. This involves counting off each square of the graph onto the canvas as you work. When a stitch or color area has been completed, draw a line through the squares that have been stitched; this will help you to keep track of your work.

Combining this use of a needlepoint graph with the method described next will make your work easier.

Tracing a design onto the canvas. After enlarging to the correct size, heavily outline the original design and place it under the canvas. With a gray indelible marker trace the design onto the canvas, ignoring the mesh formation. You can determine actual placement of stitches as you work, or you can refer back to your graphed design if you have one (see fig. 14-A).

Should you have trouble "reading" your original design through the canvas, tape the design and canvas to a window during the day and use the light to aid you in transferring your design. Then work the canvas as it is or make your stitching even easier by painting colors in the design outlines.

Painting the needlepoint canvas. The additional step of painting in the design gives you an accurate color guide to follow as you stitch. It will also make the craft more fun by alleviating some of the intense concentration necessary when you work directly from a graph.

Unless you have experience in working with oil paints, acrylic paints are the best choice for painting needlepoint canvas. They are water soluble (therefore easy to mix and to clean up) and quick to dry.

Here's what you'll need to paint on canvas: acrylic paints in colors close to those in your design, masking tape, brown wrapping paper, a drawing board or other hard surface to work on, soft pointed watercolor brushes (try sizes 1 through 4), paper towels and a container of water to clean brushes as you work, and an aluminum or plastic palette for mixing paint.

After tracing the outline of your design onto the canvas, secure it tightly with masking tape to a board covered with brown paper to absorb excess paint. Thin your paints with water until they are the consistency of thick cream. It's best to work in only one color at a time and

14-A Tracing a Design

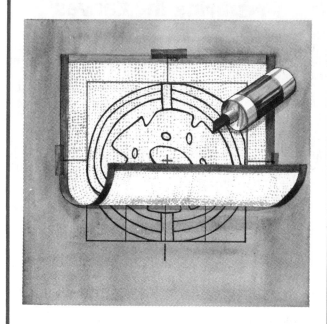

14-B Painting a Design

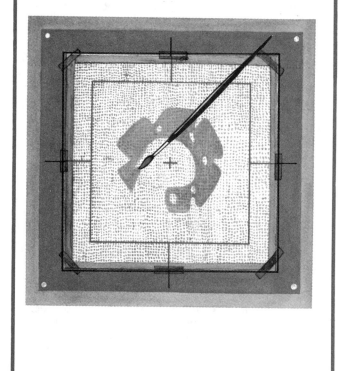

practice painting on a scrap of canvas first to check for proper paint consistency. Apply paint only to the top side of the canvas threads; don't saturate the canvas. If you find that paint seeps through to the back, thicken the paint by adding more acrylic and apply with a lighter hand.

Painting on needlepoint canvas is challenging but not really difficult after a little practice. A painted canvas makes your needlepoint more portable and convenient than working from a graph, since you don't have to be constantly referring to another source. With the basic necessities of canvas, yarn, and needle, you can stitch almost anywhere (see fig. 14-B).

While Working

Stitching a needlepoint piece takes time. To make the hours you spend most enjoyable, here are some tips from experienced needleworkers:

• Moods can manipulate the way you stitch. When you're tense and anxious, you'll pay the price in tight, unattractive stitches. Take time first to unwind and relax — for most stitchers, needlepoint becomes a refuge from the wear and tear of their busy lives. As you relax, your stitches will become smooth and even.

• The working length of a needleful of yarn must be relatively short. It is determined by the gauge of canvas: use 12 to 15 inches for finer mesh (#14 and up) and 18 to 24 inches for larger meshes (#12 and lower).

• Thread several needles before you begin to work — this allows you to stitch for a longer period without having to stop to rethread (see figs. 15-A-B).

• There are two methods for starting a length of yarn. The first method is to hold a 1-inch-long tail of yarn on the wrong side of the canvas with your finger so that you stitch over it and secure it as you work. The second method — used with the basketweave stitch — is called the "waste knot." Knot a yarn tail about 1 inch from where you want to start stitching; pull the needle from face to underside of canvas. Cut off the knot after stitching several rows (see fig. 15-C).

• To end a length of yarn, weave a tail of yarn into previously worked stitches on the wrong side of the canvas (see fig. 15-C).

• Beware of twisted yarn — as you stitch, the yarn is continually being twisted in the same direction, and you'll soon notice that the stitches are not completely covering the canvas — they will lie askew. You can prevent this by holding the canvas away from you occasionally, letting the needle and yarn hang free so the yarn can untwist itself. Another method for untwisting the yarn is to roll the needle away from you as you hold it between your thumb and index finger.

• Yarn can fray and break from the constant tug of the needle in one spot during stitching. To prevent this, it's a good idea to start with a 4-inch tail of yarn hanging from the needle and, as you work, gradually move the needle toward the end of the yarn.

• As with any needlecraft, it's important to keep both your hands and your work as clean as possible. When you're not working on it, roll your needlepoint right side in and secure it with a safety pin or piece of masking tape.

15-A Threading Your Needle

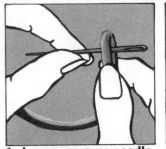

1. Loop yarn over needle

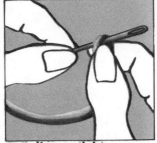

2. Pull yarn tight

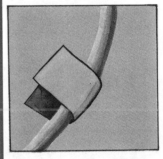

3. Remove needle

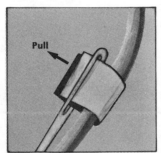

4. Force needle over yarn

15-B Paper Method

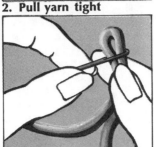

Pull

15-C Starting and Ending

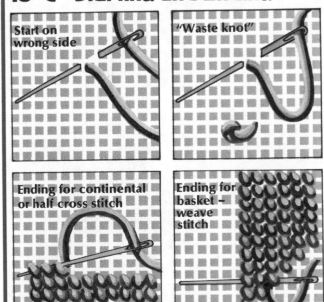

Start on wrong side

"Waste knot"

Ending for continental or half cross stitch

Ending for basket-weave stitch

Simply Stitches

More than 200 different needlepoint stitches are being worked today, most of them variations of the basic "tent" stitch, which is believed to have been developed by the early Egyptians as a means to secure their tent seams.

The basic needlepoint stitch can be worked in three different ways, all of which result in a slanting stitch covering one mesh (an intersection of threads) from lower left to upper right on the face of the canvas; the differences appear on the back of the canvas, as you will see by looking at the photos below.

Relax and concentrate on learning these stitches — once you have the half cross, continental, and basketweave at your fingertips, the seemingly awesome task of working a project will become simple.

The next 11 pages are devoted to stitches — basic, left-handed, and decorative. Study the sample stitch photographs and follow the accompanying illustrations; odd numbers indicate that the needle comes from the back of the canvas to the front, and even numbers indicate that the needle is inserted from front to back. When attempting to work decorative stitches from right-handed instructions, most left-handed stitchers find only one problem—a change in the direction in which the stitches are worked. A look at pages 18 and 19 will help to solve this difficulty.

After you've practiced the basic stitches and can do them without referring to the book, turn your attention to the decorative stitches and bargello patterns detailed on the following pages. As with any craft, practice is essential; soon you'll be working stitches easily and evenly.

Basic "Tent" Stitches

All the basic tent stitches — half cross, continental, and basketweave — create an identical surface appearance on the front.

CONTINENTAL The long diagonal thread on the wrong side of the canvas gives firm backing to a piece worked in continental stitch.

HALF CROSS Little yarn appears on the back of the canvas, making the half cross stitch a poor choice for items subject to wear.

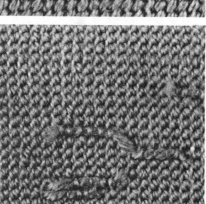

BASKETWEAVE The interwoven pattern that results on the wrong side of the canvas provides firm backing; distortion is slight.

HALF CROSS STITCH

Probably the easiest to learn and to stitch, the half cross does not cover the canvas as well as other stitches. It should be worked only on penelope canvas — because it uses less wool than the other stitches, it is less stable and needs the support of a double-threaded canvas to retain its shape. It is worked horizontally from left to right or vertically from bottom to top, which makes it a good stitch for outlining and for working small detailed areas. The canvas is turned 180° at the end of each row. The half cross will distort the canvas, but this can be corrected during blocking (see page 29).

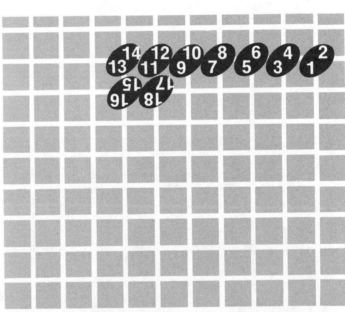

CONTINENTAL STITCH

The continental stitch produces a much firmer backing than the half cross and can be worked on all types of canvas. It, too, distorts the canvas, and sometimes a piece done in the continental stitch will require more than one blocking. Because continental is worked from right to left, the canvas is turned 180° at the end of each row. Some needlepointers consider the turning a time-consuming effort and tend to rely more on the basketweave stitch.

BASKETWEAVE STITCH

Of the basic "tent" stitches, the basketweave is the most durable and the quickest to stitch. More difficult to learn, it is worth mastering, since it's the perfect choice for working large, uncomplicated areas. You work it on the diagonal, saving time by not having to turn the canvas. The thick interlocking pattern created on the canvas back permits very little distortion.

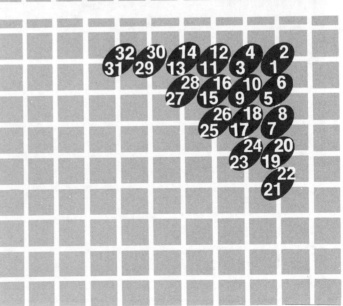

The Left-Handed Approach

The sinistral (left-handed) person was plagued in earlier centuries by society's notion that to be left-handed was in some way evil or unlucky. Though such nonsense is now recognized as being just that, the left-handed person still is inconvenienced in a generally right-hand-oriented society.

Perhaps you've haunted needlework shops and libraries in search of information dealing with needlework for left-handed people. More often than not you were probably told to hold a book either up to a mirror or upside-down. Though this would work in most cases, it's a disheartening start for the left-handed beginner who's enthusiastic about learning this exciting craft.

You want to learn needlepoint, but you're left-handed? Read on! What follows should remove the inconvenience and get you in phase for enjoying all the aspects of needlepoint.

The illustrations that follow show the sinistral approach to working the half cross, continental, and basketweave stitches. Using the stitch diagrams as guides, note that odd numbers indicate the needle coming from the back of the canvas to the front, and even numbers indicate the needle being inserted from front to back. Refer to the sample stitch photographs on the facing page to make sure your work is correct.

After you've practiced the basic stitches and can work them without referring to the book, turn your attention to the decorative stitches and bargello patterns detailed on the next nine pages. Most left-handed stitchers find only one main difference in working decorative stitches from right-handed instructions — the direction in which the stitches are worked. Some are worked in exactly the same fashion; others require changes.

Stitches that need to be altered are identified by this symbol "■", which is followed by instructions for the left-handed approach. Remember to hold the canvas in the most comfortable working position, even if this means turning the canvas 90°.

HALF CROSS STITCH

Probably the easiest to learn and to stitch, the half cross does not cover the canvas as well as other stitches. It should be worked only on penelope canvas — because it uses less wool than the other stitches, it is less stable and needs the support of a double-threaded canvas to retain its shape. It is worked horizontally from left to right or vertically from top to bottom, which makes it a good stitch for outlining and for working small detailed areas. The canvas is turned 180° at the end of each row. The half cross will distort the canvas, but this can be corrected during blocking (see page 29).

CONTINENTAL STITCH

The continental stitch produces a much firmer backing than the half cross and can be worked on all types of canvas. It, too, distorts the canvas, and sometimes a piece done in the continental stitch will require more than one blocking. Because continental is worked from left to right, the canvas is turned 180° at the end of each row. Some needlepointers consider the turning a time-consuming effort and tend to rely more on the basketweave stitch.

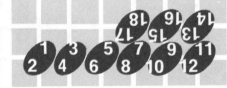

BASKETWEAVE STITCH

Of the basic "tent" stitches, the basketweave is the most durable and the quickest to stitch. More difficult to learn, it is worth mastering, since it's the perfect choice for working large, uncomplicated areas. You work it on the diagonal, saving time by not having to turn the canvas. The thick interlocking pattern created on the canvas back permits very little distortion.

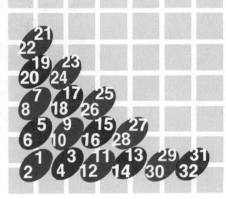

Decorative Stitches

Mastering the basic stitches is fundamental if you expect to enjoy needlepoint. But, like the painter given only one tube of paint, you may begin to crave some variety. The next eight pages will help you expand your "palette" of stitches.

Using the illustrations and stitch sample photos that follow, practice the decorative stitches until you no longer need to look.

This symbol "✳" appearing with an illustration means that you turn the canvas 180° at the end of each row; then continue stitching.

Different stitches have different wearing qualities, and these are noted in many of the descriptions that follow. Generally, the longer the stitch, the less resistant to wear and tear.

Keep in mind that for certain stitches (Gobelin, satin, and triangle, for example) you must use more strands of yarn to cover the canvas adequately.

Special left-handed instructions are indicated by this symbol — ■.

CROSS STITCH

On penelope or leno canvas, work a row of half cross stitches from left to right; then return from right to left, "crossing" all the stitches in the same direction. On mono canvas, work each stitch as a complete unit; when you finish a row, turn the canvas 180° and stitch the next row.

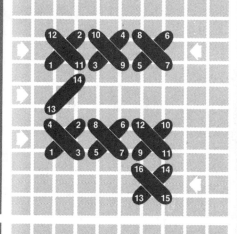

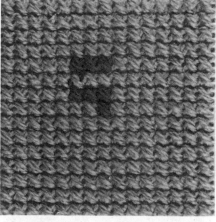

UPRIGHT CROSS STITCH

Sometimes called the Greek cross, this stitch is very durable and works up quickly on all types of canvas. Complete each stitch individually, always crossing in the same direction, before moving to the next stitch. ■ Turn canvas 180° at end of each row.

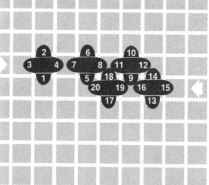

DOUBLE CROSS STITCH

A combination of large cross stitches surrounding small upright crosses, the double cross is quick to stitch and very effective worked in two colors. Be sure to use enough strands of yarn to cover the canvas well. This is a durable stitch. ■ Work from bottom to top.

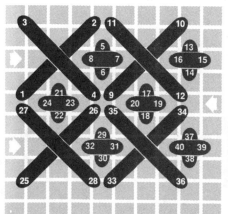

OBLONG CROSS WITH BACKSTITCH

A very interesting texture is created by this durable stitch, but it is slow to work and uses a lot of wool. Being an upright stitch, it will distort the canvas very little.
■ Work from bottom to top.

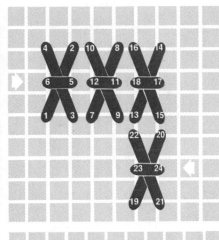

SMYRNA CROSS STITCH

Slow to work, the long-wearing Smyrna cross stitch has a distinctive bumpy look that's effective as a single accent stitch. Work each stitch separately, as all must cross in the same direction.
■ Work from bottom to top and left to right.

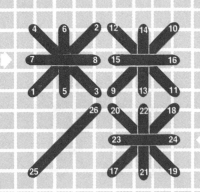

DOUBLE LEVIATHAN STITCH

Similar to the Smyrna cross but larger and bumpier, this stitch is faster to work up because it is done over four canvas threads in each direction. Like the Smyrna, this stitch is very effective when used singly as an accent.

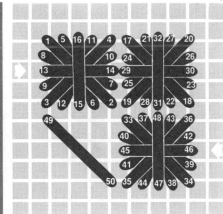

UPRIGHT OR SLANTED GOBELIN STITCH

Worked in horizontal rows over two to six canvas threads, these are both quick to stitch. For the slanted gobelin, merely lean the stitch to the right, crossing one to four vertical threads as well. Both tend to snag if stitched too long. Keep the yarn full and untwisted.

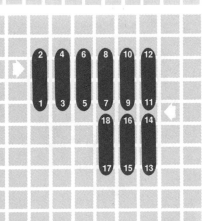

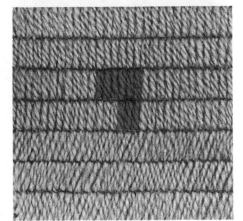

SPLIT GOBELIN STITCH

You start with a row of straight Gobelin stitches. For succeeding rows, each stitch pierces the one immediately above, and is completed over the same or a different number of threads. Stronger than the upright, the split Gobelin gives a woven effect.

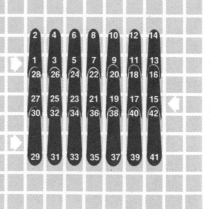

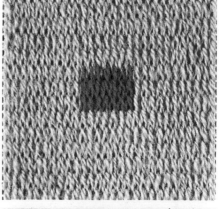

MOSAIC STITCH

One long and two short stitches combine to form a small square; these squares work up quickly and can be used in any part of a design for slight textural variations. Don't pull the yarn too tight or it will distort the canvas. This stitch has a firm backing.
■ Work from top to bottom and left to right.

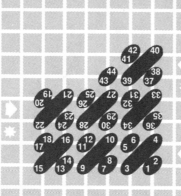

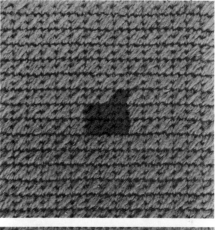

CASHMERE STITCH

Add a second long stitch to the mosaic and you have the cashmere stitch. It's a bit too large for detailed work, but this quick stitch makes a handsome border or background stitch. Again, be careful not to pull the yarn too tight, as it can distort the canvas. This stitch is long-wearing.
■ Reverse even and odd numbers.

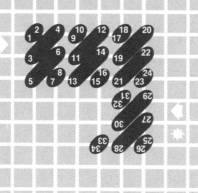

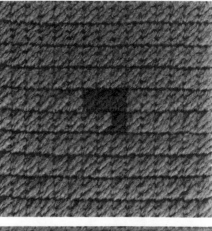

DIAGONAL CASHMERE STITCH

Also a quick and durable stitch, the diagonal cashmere is not as defined as the other geometric stitches illustrated. It is an excellent choice for backgrounds.
■ Reverse even and odd numbers.

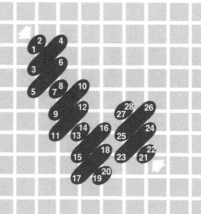

PARISIAN STITCH

The long-lasting Parisian works up quickly into an interesting geometric pattern. Because it is stitched upright rather than over canvas thread intersections, you must be sure to use enough strands to cover the canvas completely. Experiment with different colors in each row.
■ Reverse even and odd numbers.

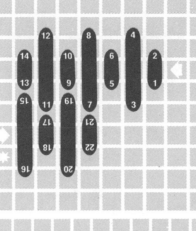

DIAGONAL PARISIAN OR DIAGONAL MOSAIC

This is a quick stitch that can be worked either like the basketweave or diagonally in separate rows from lower right to upper left. Its firm backing makes it very durable. ■ Work from lower left to upper right.

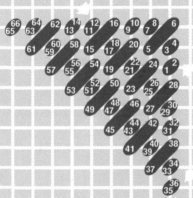

SCOTCH STITCH

A versatile extension of the mosaic, yet not as firm, the Scotch can add textural interest to a design or can be used as a background. Shown here with five stitches per "stitch," it can also be worked in seven per "stitch." You can work horizontally or diagonally, but don't pull the yarn too tight.

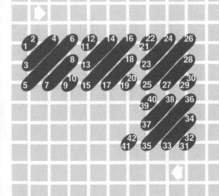

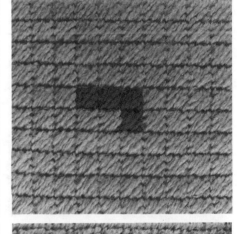

SCOTCH STITCH VARIATION I

By outlining each Scotch stitch with half cross stitches, you can add subtle texture to certain areas of your piece. Work entirely in one color, or use a second color for outlining.

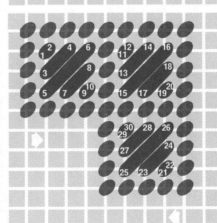

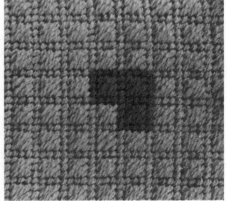

Special left-handed instructions are indicated by this symbol — ■.

SCOTCH STITCH VARIATION II

Squares of Scotch stitches alternated with continental or half cross create this attractive checkerboard pattern. It works well in one color, but two colors make the checkerboard more pronounced.

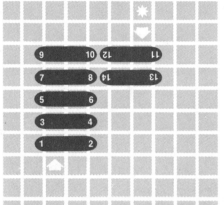

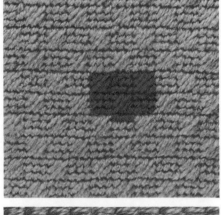

SATIN STITCH

Worked like the upright Gobelin, the satin stitch covers vertical threads rather than horizontal ones. Remember, though — the larger the stitch, the more likely it is to snag, making this stitch less durable than others. ■ Reverse even and odd numbers.

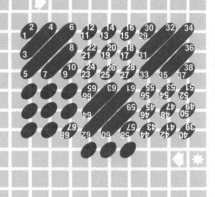

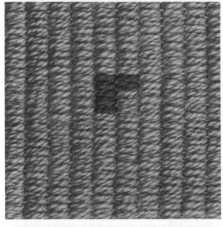

BRICK STITCH

Also a derivation of the upright Gobelin, the long-wearing brick stitch is worked over two to four horizontal or vertical threads in a half drop formation resembling a brick wall. The "bricks" can also be groups of stitches in equal numbers. ■ Work from right to left, then left to right.

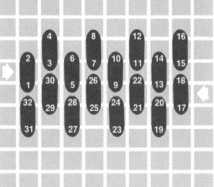

FLAME STITCH

The flame is like the Gobelin, with this exception — rather than appearing in even rows, the flame stitch is worked over horizontal threads in a zigzag or "flame" pattern. It works up very quickly and is fun to stitch in rows of variegated colors. Be sure to keep the yarn full and untwisted. ■ Work from right to left, then from left to right.

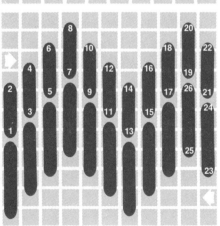

TRIANGLE STITCH

In this bargello variation, four triangles are stitched together to form a square with small cross stitches at the corners; it has a firm backing. Quick to work up, this geometric stitch is striking when used singly.

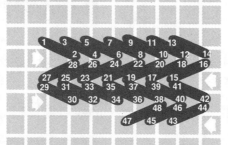

BYZANTINE STITCH

Though it looks complicated, the Byzantine stitch works up quickly after the first row is established; then, just follow the "steps" you've stitched. Worked in one color or in several, these zigzag stripes make a dramatic border or background of durable stitches.
■ Reverse even and odd numbers.

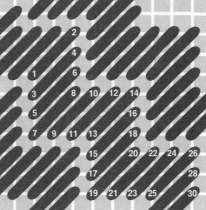

KNITTING STITCH

Good-looking and sturdy, yet slow to do, the knitting stitch is handsome in small background areas. It is a very tight stitch and requires more wool than other stitches similar in size. Work horizontally from left to right, then back from right to left.

KALEM STITCH

This stitch is like the knitting stitch except that the kalem is worked vertically rather than horizontally. The striped, braided look that results is very effective.

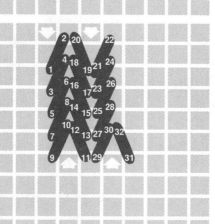

Special left-handed instructions are indicated by this symbol — ■.

Briefly Bargello

Bargello stitchery — upright stitches worked in repeat patterns over 2 to 6 horizontal canvas threads — usually appears in several shades of one color. Sometimes called Florentine embroidery, flame stitch, or Hungarian point, bargello is one of the oldest known forms of canvas embroidery.

Florentine, brick, and Gobelin stitches are all used in bargello work. Because the stitches don't cross canvas thread intersections, there is practically no canvas distortion, and most bargello pieces need only be blocked with a steam iron.

While working bargello patterns, be sure the yarn covers the canvas completely; the yarn should not be pulled too tight or twisted. Read about bargello canvas on page 6 and then try the patterns illustrated below; you might also try experimenting with patterns and colors of your own. Bargello work is fast.
Bargello designs: Barbara Di Conza.

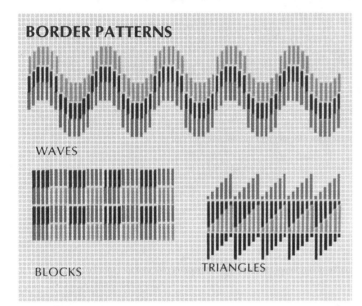

BORDER PATTERNS

WAVES

BLOCKS

TRIANGLES

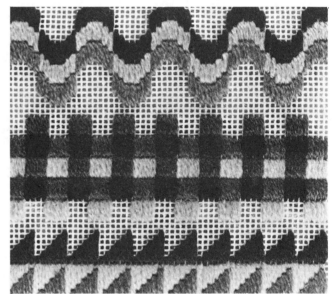

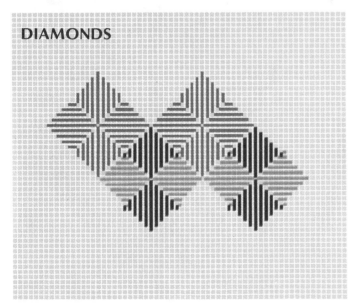

DIAMONDS

ARROWS

SPIRALS

MEDALLION

Designs-Personally Yours

If you've yearned to design a needlepoint piece, but never felt quite sure you had the stuff original stitches are made of — take heart. A few simple design and color guidelines, along with the desire to create something with a personal touch, are all you need to get started stitching your own projects.

Choosing Your Design

What do you want to look at during hours of stitching and for years afterward? This may seem like an idle question, but if you choose a design of many colors with great detail, you may grow tired of it before you even finish it, particularly if it's your first project. Because of needlepoint's lasting quality, many stitchers choose designs and colors that have classic and timeless themes.

If you keep your eyes open, you'll notice that potential resources for designs are everywhere. For example, greeting cards, magazine advertisements, seed catalogs, record jackets, photo calendars, and china patterns are only a few sources of simple, colorful motifs from which an entire design or portions thereof may be adapted for needlepoint. Consider a single flower from a larger floral design, or a small area taken from a big, vivid geometric pattern — either of these could be worked into a handsome needlepoint piece. From such overall patterns you can create coordinated needlepoint projects to complement your decor.

Note that nature, too, abounds with design ideas; abstractions of the flora and fauna around us often give a fresh twist to the commonplace.

A good rule of thumb when you set out to design your first needlepoint project is to keep it simple. Apply this rule to such elements as project size, yarn colors, needlepoint stitches, and even actual design motifs. Don't get involved with a design too complicated to finish; it will only lead to frustration.

Avoid intricate patterns with many curved areas if you're a beginner; these are difficult to interpret in needlepoint stitches. Because needlepoint canvas is a grid-like foundation, curved lines are actually reproduced as a series of steps. You can create an impression of roundness by stitching on fine-mesh canvas.

Working in petit point stitches will enable you to capture precise design features, as our artist has done for the Hopi Indian Eyeglass Case (page 48), which is worked on #18 mono canvas. Remember, though, that this project measures only 7 inches square — a larger piece could become a very tedious task. Instead, try using penelope canvas on which you can combine petit point and gros point stitches to obtain fine detail in specific areas of your design (see close-up of butterfly on page 33).

When designing for needlepoint, keep in mind another point: texture. The needleworker can indulge in some 200 decorative stitches to effectively create subtle surface changes (study Victorian House on page 44 to see how it's done). However, if you're not an experienced needleworker, take care not to become carried away with the possibilities at hand. Try using only one or two decorative stitches at first to enrich a background or to emphasize a specific design area (for an example, see the border around Parrot Parade, page 37). Remember the architectural maxim "less is more"; simplicity leads to a more tasteful end product.

To transform your design idea into a handsome needlepoint piece, read the sections regarding design enlargement and transfer on page 12; there you'll find a variety of ways for getting from sketch to stitch.

Having pondered the above thoughts on design, now focus your attention on color — as it can make or break your design.

Color-Your Trademark

By relating an individual's color sense to that individual's personality traits, psychologists have repeatedly tried to pinpoint why certain people prefer certain colors. Whether or not such things can ever be determined, it's true that your color preferences are a matter of personal taste and often become your trademark.

There is practically no limit to the choice of needlepoint yarn colors available to you. If you're a beginner, though, you'd be wise to start with only a few colors and work up gradually to an expanded palette.

You may be initially overwhelmed by the enormous selection of colors available in needlepoint yarns. That selection will probably be both a happy discovery and a warning that a pleasing arrangement of colors will take careful consideration and planning. Remember that with color, as with design, simplicity is the key to success.

Choose all your colors at one time. Hold them up together to see if you like the combination. Then try several other combinations of colors; you might hit upon an ideal arrangement that you hadn't considered before.

Don't be shy with bright colors. After stitching, the brightness of such colors tends to dull slightly. Used next to one another, bright colors will cancel some of each other's brightness. On the other hand, if you want to draw attention to a bright color area, surround or border it with black or another dark color.

When selecting colors for needlepoint, consider contrasts. Colors that seem to have sufficient contrast to "read" visually as two separate shades when held up to the light, may well blend completely into one another when stitched in adjacent areas, particularly in a monochromatic color scheme. If this is the effect you want, fine. Such close shading is often used in bargello work (see the Bargello Typewriter Cover, page 78), to enhance the rhythmical flow of its repeat patterns. But if you want crisp, clear definitions of color, it is necessary to select shades with a definite contrast.

You may wish to research the areas of design and color more thoroughly; if so, visit your local library, where you'll find books dealing solely with design and color.

General Finishing Techniques

For finishing needlepoint pieces, some techniques are universal, such as the blocking of your completed canvas and the creation and application of welting, tassels, loops, ties, and twisted cord trim during finishing procedures. The information that follows includes step-by-step directions for accomplishing each of these techniques. Detailed instructions for finishing specific needlepoint articles appear in the projects section of this book.

Blocking for Needlepoint

After stitching, your needlepoint will no doubt be at least slightly pulled out of shape and will require blocking. Blocking a small or medium-size needlepoint piece is a fairly simple procedure, and doing it yourself will save you the expense of having it done professionally; large pieces, though, may need to be blocked by a professional.

To block a needlepoint piece at home you'll need these: aluminum or copper pushpins or a staple gun, a firm blocking board (an old drawing board or a piece of plywood will do nicely), a draftsman's triangle or right angle, white vinegar, pliers and C-clamps (both optional), rabbit skin glue (can be purchased at art supply or needlework shops), and the brown paper outline of the canvas you drew before stitching (see page 13).

1. Fasten brown paper outline to board.
2. Secure board to a table with C-clamps (optional, but clamps will keep the blocking board stable while you're pulling on the canvas).
3. With a mixture of 2 to 3 tablespoons of white vinegar and 1 to 2 cups of water, sponge both sides of needlepoint until entire piece is damp but not saturated. Vinegar and water help to "set" yarn colors (see fig. 29-A).
4. Place needlepoint *face down* on board and begin to tack or staple about 1 inch from stitched area, aligning edges of canvas with outline drawn on brown paper. Begin by tacking at center of each side and working out to corners, stretching needlepoint into shape as you go. To get a really good grip, use pliers to grasp edge of canvas while pulling it back to shape. You'll need to tack about every inch or half-inch to hold canvas securely in place (see fig. 29-B).
5. Sponge needlepoint again, if it has begun to dry.
6. In a warm, dry spot, lay blocked needlepoint flat until it is completely dry (24 hours or longer).
7. While blocked needlepoint is drying, prepare rabbit skin glue: Bring 2 cups of water to a boil, add 1 ounce of glue, and stir until dissolved. Remove from heat and continue stirring constantly until mixture reaches room temperature. Refrigerate for 8 to 10 hours or until mixture reaches consistency of gelatin.
8. Spread a small amount of glue onto back of needlepoint with your hands (glue washes off with soap and water). Using a spatula or butter knife, scrape off any excess glue; only a thin film should remain. This procedure will stabilize your piece and will help to hold its shape (see fig. 29-C).

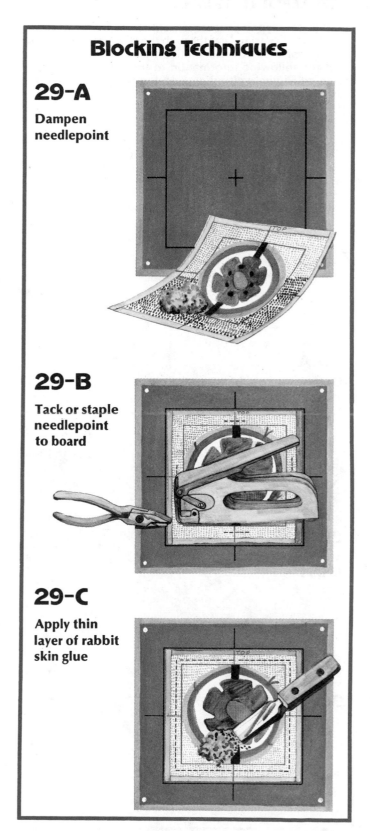

Blocking Techniques

29-A
Dampen needlepoint

29-B
Tack or staple needlepoint to board

29-C
Apply thin layer of rabbit skin glue

9. Allow needlepoint to dry an additional 24 hours; then remove from board. If any glue seeps through to front of needlepoint, sponge it off with a damp cloth. Your piece is now ready to be finished.

NEEDLEPOINT TRIMS

Certain needlepoint pieces are enhanced by the addition of a decorative trim. Leaf through the projects in this book for examples of how decorative trim can be used; then read the following information to find out how you can make your own welting, tassels, loops, ties, and twisted cord trim.

How to Make Welting

Though you can purchase ready-made welting (sometimes called "corded" welting) in the notions department of most fabric stores, it may be difficult to find a color or texture compatible with your needlepoint. Rather than do without, make your own welting — you'll find it's easy.

Welting is made by encasing purchased cord in a strip of bias-cut fabric (bias-cut means that you cut the strips on a 45° angle to the straight grain of the fabric — this is called the true bias; see fig. 30-A).

First choose a fabric that will complement your needlepoint in both color and texture. If you intend to back the needlepoint piece, as for a pillow, make your welting from the same fabric as the backing; or you could choose a fabric of contrasting color as a design accent.

1. Measure length of seam into which welting will be sewn and then add 4 inches to determine total length of welting you need to make.

2. Fold fabric diagonally as shown in figure 30-A and pin to hold in place. Cut fabric along fold and remove pins and fabric triangle. To determine the number of bias strips to cut, measure length of diagonal edge; then divide this measurement into the total length you need, allowing for ½-inch seam allowance for each bias seam.

3. Width of fabric strip is determined by cord diameter — three times the diameter of the cord plus an additional 1¼ inches for seam allowance. Since most needlepoint projects require welting made with ¼-inch-diameter cord, 2-inch-wide bias fabric strips will be adequate for most of your work.

Starting at diagonally cut edge of cloth, mark off with tailor's chalk parallel lines spaced 2 inches apart. Also mark along both top and bottom edges of diagonally cut fabric a ¼-inch seam allowance for joining bias strips (see fig. 30-B).

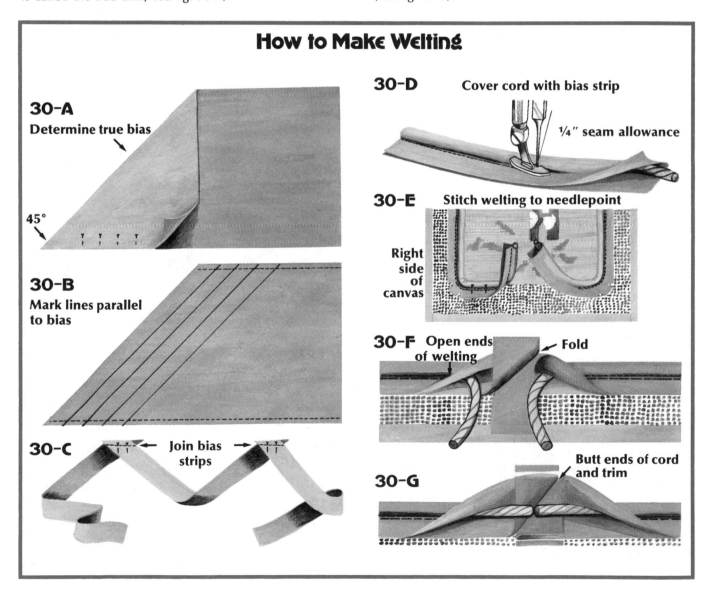

How to Make Welting

30-A Determine true bias

45°

30-B Mark lines parallel to bias

30-C ← Join bias strips →

30-D Cover cord with bias strip

¼" seam allowance

30-E Stitch welting to needlepoint

Right side of canvas

30-F Open ends of welting — Fold

30-G Butt ends of cord and trim

4. Cut fabric strips apart; then pin with right sides together as shown in figure 30-C and machine stitch ¼ inch in from raw edges. Continue to join fabric strips until you have enough to make welting in the length desired.

5. Cut a piece of cord the same length as fabric strip; then center cord on wrong side of strip. Fold fabric strip around cord, wrong sides together, and pin to hold. With a zipper foot, machine baste (8 stitches to the inch) close to, but not directly against, cord (see fig. 30-D).

6. Stitch welting to right side of needlepoint piece as shown in figure 30-E, leaving 4 inches free at each end for joining welting ends. Remove from sewing machine.

7. Remove 4 inches of machine basting stitches from each end of welting and then open ends of fabric (see fig. 30-F). Fold each end of fabric strip as shown. Foldlines should meet exactly. Mark foldlines with chalk, pin together, and stitch. Trim seam and press open. Trim ends of cord so that ends meet exactly (see fig. 30-G). Fold fabric over cord and continue stitching.

Yarn Tassels

You make these by wrapping yarn around a 3-inch square of cardboard 30 or 40 times — enough for a plump tassel. With a separate piece of yarn, tie strands together tightly at one edge of cardboard. Cut other end free from cardboard (see fig. 31-A); then, about 1 inch down from tie, wrap entire bundle with a separate strand of yarn and secure ends as shown in figure 31-B.

Loops and Ties

Make these simply and quickly with turned or corded fabric strips. Cut a 1-inch-wide piece of fabric to the length you need. With right sides together, fold in half lengthwise and, using 12 stitches per inch, stitch across one short end, then along the raw edges the length of the tie. Trim close to stitching. With eraser end of a pencil or similar tool, turn tie right side out (see fig. 31-C). Turn open end in and stitch closed.

If you want a corded tie, cut a length of cord twice as long as the length you need. At midpoint of cord, wrap fabric strip (right side in) around cord and stitch as shown in figure 31-D. Trim close to stitching. Holding end of encased cord, pull fabric casing down over free end of cord (see fig. 31-E). Turn open end in and stitch closed. Trim away excess cord.

Twisted Cord Trim

It takes two people to make this trim, as well as two pencils and a piece of yarn 7½ times the finished length of twisted cord you wish to make.

Tie one end of the length of yarn to the center of the pencil you're holding; then loop the yarn over the pencil the other person is holding, over your pencil again, and then back to the second pencil. You now have three threads of equal length stretched between the two pencils. Tie the free end of the yarn to the second pencil (see fig. 31-F).

Twist the pencils in opposite directions until the yarn starts to kink near each pencil. Grasp the center point of the twisted yarn and pass your pencil to the other person, who holds the two pencils close together. Keep the yarn taut throughout this procedure, holding it at the center with two hands. Now let go of the yarn with the hand closest to the end and, using this free hand as a guide, allow the yarn to twist over itself (see fig. 31-G).

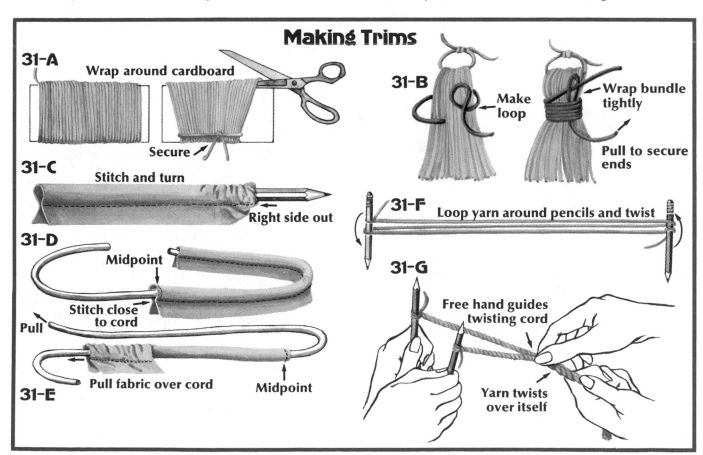

Making Trims

31-A Wrap around cardboard — Secure

31-B Make loop — Wrap bundle tightly — Pull to secure ends

31-C Stitch and turn — Right side out

31-D Midpoint — Stitch close to cord — Pull

31-E Pull fabric over cord — Midpoint

31-F Loop yarn around pencils and twist

31-G Free hand guides twisting cord — Yarn twists over itself

Projects: Start to Finish

INSTRUCTIONS for "Cows in Clover" (top) begin on page 52. Graph for "Hopi Indian Clutch" (bottom) is on page 50; entire project (including an accompanying eyeglass case) begins on page 48.

More than likely you've turned to this section before reading what precedes it. After all, aren't the actual projects the crux of any craft?

Before You Begin

Skim through the next 47 pages — you'll find the projects illustrated with photos and needlepoint graphs, all in full color. Chosen to appeal to a wide variety of tastes and abilities, our designs are meant to stir a desire on your part to learn needlepoint — or to rekindle an old affair with this elegant craft.

Complete how-to instructions take you from bare canvas to finished project, and adjacent art spots clearly illustrate special techniques. Before beginning any project, read all instructions carefully for an overall idea of what to expect.

A Stitch Guide and Yarn Count accompanies every project, telling you what stitches you'll use and how much of each yarn color you'll need. But before you go off to buy yarn and canvas, familiarize yourself with needlepoint materials, stitches, and working techniques (see pages 4–31).

If you're a beginner, master at least the basic stitches before attempting a project; the first part of this book explains all you need to know to get started. (Even if you're an experienced needleworker, you are likely to find an informative tidbit or a new decorative stitch to try.) Then when you've achieved a basic technical grasp, return to the projects section — your fingers should be itching for stitching.

The pattern graphs in this book are grid patterns of colored squares that have been reduced in size from the actual canvas size. Each square on a graph represents one mesh (or intersection) of canvas threads. The grids are further divided by bolder lines that indicate the gauge of the canvas and help you to keep your place while stitching. For instance, the graph for Parrot Parade Pillow on page 38 has bold lines every seventh square; this means it is to be worked on #7 canvas. The bold lines actually indicate 1 square inch of working area.

If you intend to work directly from the graph, it might be wise to draw a grid pattern of lines spaced 1 inch apart on your canvas, too, using a gray indelible marker; these lines will relate directly to the bold lines on the grid. Refer to pages 12–15 for how-to instructions on enlarging and tracing or painting a design onto canvas.

You'll notice that the graphs for certain projects have been split and appear on two pages. The split graphs create no problem for the stitcher. When you enlarge these designs, merely butt the split edges together exactly to make one complete graph. If you work on these projects directly from the graphs in the book, just continue stitching each row as if there were no break in the graph. When working directly from a graph, it's a good idea to cross out areas on the graph that you've already stitched.

A Final Thought

Needlepoint is a personal craft, and projects can be altered to suit your taste. Try substituting stitches; change colors if you like; stitch a tote bag design but finish it as a pillow instead. For example, the Pussy Willow Tote on page 75 could be a large pillow; the Bargello Typewriter Cover on page 78 would be as handsome as a carryall tote in shades of blue or green.

It's wise to test color or stitch adaptations on a scrap of canvas first to be sure the effect is what you want. As you become increasingly adept in needlepoint, you'll find that experimenting with materials, stitches, and techniques — even designing your own projects (see page 28) — can add new dimensions to this very appealing craft.

Choose a project that matches your ability; for instance, the fairly complex Strawberry Basket on pages 72–73 should not be a "first" project. The beginner would do well to choose something less taxing. Before you start a project, read all instructions thoroughly; when buying materials, don't skimp on amounts or quality; as you work, aim for smooth, even stitches; and most of all — have fun.

THIS COLLAGE includes tidbits from the following projects:
A. "Pussy Willow Tote," page 75
B. "Parrot Parade," page 37
C. "Positively Poppies," page 61
D. "Cereal Box Pillow," page 54
E. "Angel Baby," page 69
F. "Bear Hugs," page 46
G. "Victorian House," page 44

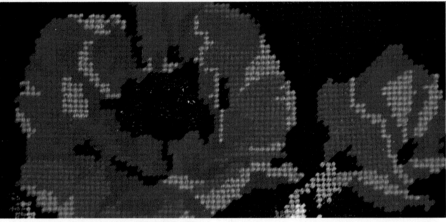

B

C

D

E

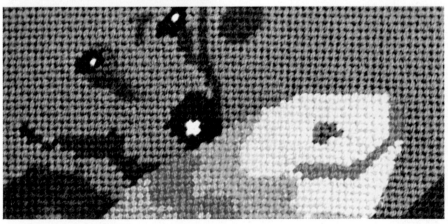

F

G

A Handy Twosome

If you're a beginner who's just mastered the basic needlepoint stitches — basketweave and continental — try them out on these two simple, practical projects.

Here's your chance to practice working basketweave stitches into a curved area. Though the circle is usually considered a difficult shape to stitch accurately, notice that the bands around the flower and petals are not perfectly round, so slight variations in stitch placement will go unnoticed. You'll also have an opportunity to learn the fast and easy slanted Gobelin.

This handy twosome will be finished before you know it. Meanwhile, you'll have gained not only these useful sewing accessories but also a sense of accomplishment and the confidence to tackle more difficult projects.

Design: Diane Tapscott.

PINCUSHION

1. Enlarge design according to directions on page 12.
2. Bind an 8-inch square of #12 mono or leno canvas with masking tape. Draw outline of canvas on brown paper and mark as shown on page 13.
3. With a gray indelible marker and a compass, draw a 4½-inch-diameter circle centered on the square. There will be a 1¾-inch border of canvas all around.
4. Trace design onto canvas within drawn circle, or work directly from pincushion graph.
5. Stitch purple spots in flower center first, using basketweave or continental stitch, with 1 full thread of Persian yarn in a #18 tapestry needle.
6. Continue stitching from center, out toward edges.
7. Block as shown on page 29.

SCISSORS CASE

1. Enlarge design according to directions on page 12.
2. Bind edges of a 6 by 16-inch piece of #12 mono or leno canvas with masking tape. Draw outline of canvas on brown paper and mark as shown on page 13.
3. With a gray indelible marker, draw a 2½ by 12½-inch rectangle on canvas.
4. Trace design onto canvas with indelible marker, or work directly from graph.
5. Stitch flower centers and petals first, using basketweave or continental stitch, with 1 full thread of Persian yarn in a #18 tapestry needle.
6. Stitch stripes in slanted Gobelin (see page 21) over 3 vertical canvas threads, using 1 full thread of Persian yarn.
7. Fill in white background with basketweave stitch, using 2 strands from a thread of Persian yarn.
8. Block according to directions on page 29.

(Continued on page 36)

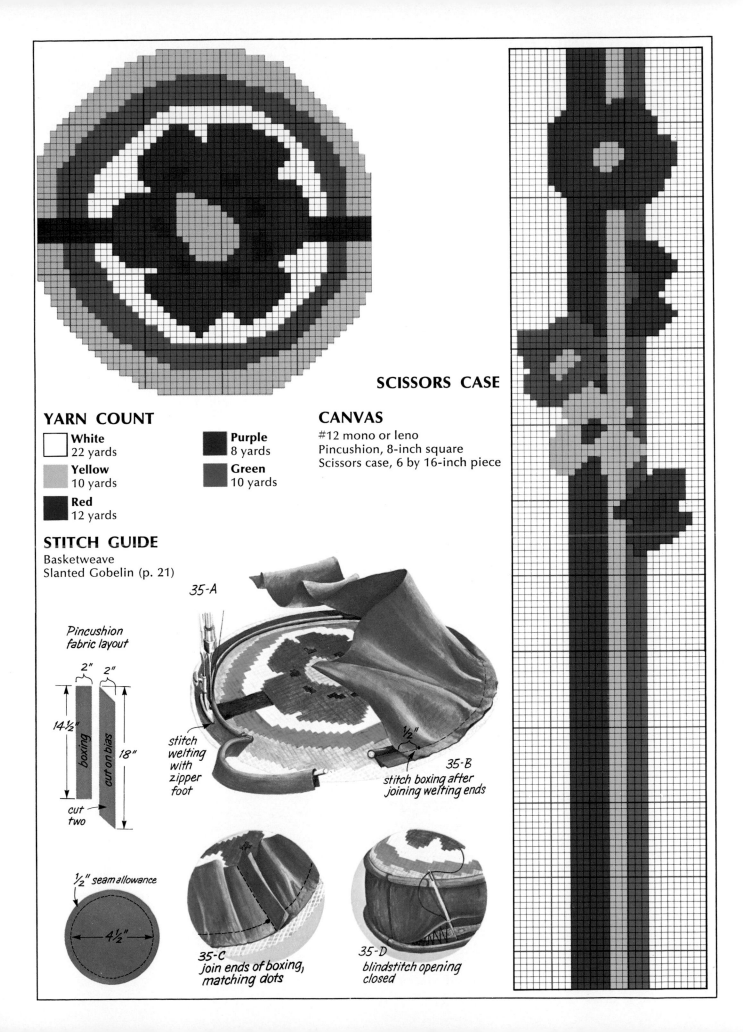

YARN COUNT

White
22 yards

Yellow
10 yards

Red
12 yards

Purple
8 yards

Green
10 yards

STITCH GUIDE
Basketweave
Slanted Gobelin (p. 21)

SCISSORS CASE

CANVAS
#12 mono or leno
Pincushion, 8-inch square
Scissors case, 6 by 16-inch piece

Pincushion
fabric layout

2"   2"

14½"

boxing

cut on bias

18"

cut
two

½" seam allowance

4½"

35-A

stitch
welting
with
zipper
foot

½"

35-B
stitch boxing after
joining welting ends

35-C
join ends of boxing,
matching dots

35-D
blindstitch opening
closed

FINISHING TECHNIQUES

You'll need: For cutting all pattern pieces, ½ yard of 36-inch-wide red velveteen (see layout). **Pincushion**—matching thread, clear nylon sewing thread, 1 yard of ¼-inch-diameter cord for welting; bird cage gravel for stuffing. **Scissors Case** — matching thread, curved upholsterer's needle, white glue, 17 inches twisted cord trim (see page 31).

Pincushion

1. After blocking, machine stitch 2 rows through canvas around edges of needlepoint; remove binding.
2. Cut out backing, boxing, and welting according to pattern layout on page 35. Trim canvas to ½ inch.
3. Following directions on page 30, make two 18-inch-long pieces of welting.
4. Sew 1 piece of welting to needlepoint (see fig. 35-A), using zipper foot. Follow directions on page 31 for closing ends of welting.
5. Sew remaining piece of welting to back of pincushion.
6. Stitch boxing to needlepoint, starting at dot (see fig. 35-B).
7. Join ends of boxing with ½ inch seam allowance, matching dots (see fig. 35-C); press seam open.
8. Stitch backing to boxing, leaving 2 inches open.
9. Turn needlepoint right side out and stuff until plump.
10. Blindstitch opening closed (see fig. 35-D).

Scissors Case

1. After blocking, machine stitch 2 rows through canvas around edges of needlepoint to prevent canvas threads from raveling; remove binding.
2. Cut out lining 6 by 16 inches on straight of grain; then pin lining to needlepoint, right sides together.

3. Machine stitch across bottom of piece and 1½ inches up each side, through last 2 rows of needlepoint stitches to prevent canvas threads from raveling (see fig. 36-A).
4. Trim fabric and excess canvas to ½ inch. Also trim stitched corners diagonally (see fig. 36-A).
5. Turn right side out.
6. Fold down and glue 3 canvas edges, mitering corners (see fig. 36-B).
7. Apply small amount of glue all over wrong side of needlepoint canvas.
8. Pull lining fabric over glued side of needlepoint tightly to allow for eventual fold in piece.
9. Trim excess lining fabric to edge of stitched area.
10. Fold at line A (see fig. 36-C).
11. Handstitch 2 sides of needlepoint, using curved upholsterer's needle and clear nylon sewing thread (see fig. 36-D).
12. Attach twisted cord trim, using blind handstitches (see fig. 36-D).
13. Sew on snap by hand.

Project Variations

• Don't stuff the pincushion; instead make four, six, or eight coasters for cool summer drinks. To finish the coasters, use the instructions on page 41.
• To fashion a belt, eliminate rows of stitches on both sides of the scissors case, narrowing it to 1½ inches. Extend the stripes at each end until the belt is equal to your waist measurement. Now just add a buckle.
• To make a case for your dressmaker's shears, try stitching on a canvas of larger mesh, perhaps #7. The borders may still have to be extended to fit. Also, you'll have to use more strands of yarn in your needle to cover the larger mesh.

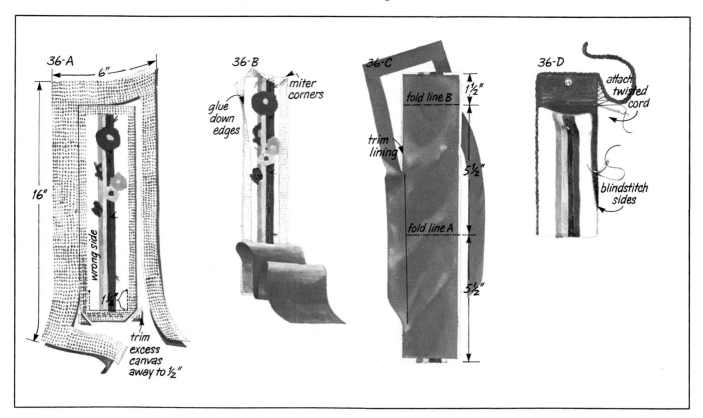

36-A 6" 16" *wrong side* 1½" *trim excess canvas away to ½"*

36-B *miter corners* *glue down edges*

36-C *fold line B* 1½" *trim lining* 5½" *fold line A* 5½"

36-D *attach twisted cord* *blindstitch sides*

Parrot Parade

Close your eyes. Imagine you are sun-bathing on a tropical isle — warm sea breezes, salt air, and the amusing conversations of parrots waft through the palms above.

You can bring home a bit of this fantasy by stitching this brilliantly colored box pillow we call "Parrot Parade." The parrots are worked in the basketweave stitch and surrounded by a frame of mosaic stitch. This large pillow is stitched on #7 canvas with doubled threads of Persian yarn and tripled threads of tapestry wool.

Design: Diane Tapscott.

1. Enlarge design according to directions on page 12.
2. Bind edges of 21 by 23-inch piece of #7 (rug-type) canvas with masking tape. Draw outline of canvas on brown paper and mark as shown on page 13.
3. Draw a 17 by 19-inch rectangle on canvas with a gray indelible marker leaving a 2-inch border all around.
4. Work from stitch graph or draw enlarged design directly onto canvas, using indelible marker.
5. Stitch parrots and branch first in basketweave or continental, using 6 strands of Persian yarn (1 full thread, doubled) in a #16 tapestry needle.
6. Stitch green leaves in basketweave, using 3 full threads of tapestry wool in a #16 tapestry needle.
7. Complete inner design area in basketweave with sky blue, using 6 strands of Persian yarn.
8. Using 6 strands of Persian yarn, stitch frame in mosaic (see page 22), filling in with continental stitch where necessary around leaves.
9. To make finishing easier, work satin stitch over 3 threads all the way around needlepointed area (do this with leftover yarn, as it won't show after finishing).
10. Block according to directions on page 29.

FINISHING TECHNIQUES

You'll need: 38 inches of 45-inch-wide light brown velveteen for backing, boxing, and welting (see fabric pattern layout 39-A); matching thread; 13 feet of ¼-inch-diameter cord for welting; clear nylon thread and sewing needle; polyester batting for stuffing; 27¼ inches of 36-inch-wide muslin for inner pillow (see fabric layout 39-A).

Inner Pillow

1. Cut 2 pieces of muslin, *each* 17¾ by 19¾ inches; mark ½-inch seamline with pencil.
2. Cut 2 muslin strips, *each* 2¾ by 37½ inches.
3. Join ends of strips with ¼-inch seam allowance; press seams open. This gives one 71-inch-long continuous band.
4. Find centers of 17¾-inch sides of muslin rectangle by folding in half; mark centers and corners with pencil dots on seamline.
5. Matching boxing seam to center dot, stitch boxing to one rectangle, ½ inch from raw edge (fig. 39-B).
6. Pivot at corner dot and continue stitching; clip corners as you sew (fig. 39-C).
7. Stitch all the way around and back to first dot; trim seam and press open.
8. Pin remaining rectangle of muslin to boxing and stitch ½ inch in from raw edge, leaving a 6-inch opening; trim

seam and press open.
9. Turn right side out and stuff with polyester batting.
10. Push polyester away from raw edges and secure with pins (see fig. 43-A, page 43).
11. Turn in raw edges ½ inch and machine stitch closed.

Pillow Cover

1. After blocking, machine stitch 2 rows through canvas around edges of needlepointed area to prevent canvas threads from raveling; remove binding and trim excess canvas to ¾ inch all around.
2. Cut backing and boxing for pillow cover (see fig. 39-A). Mark seams, centers, and corners on back of fabric.
3. Cut bias strips and make two 76-inch lengths of welting (see fig. 39-A) according to directions on page 30.
4. Using zipper foot, stitch 1 length of welting to needlepoint and one length to backing (see fig. 39-D), joining ends as shown on page 30. Clip corners.
5. Stitch *all* ends of boxing together with ¼-inch seam allowance, right sides together; press seams open.
6. With right sides together, pin boxing to needlepoint.
7. Stitch all around through needlepoint, welting, and boxing, using zipper foot and following seamline where welting and needlepoint are joined.
8. Pin backing to boxing; stitch 3 sides together (fig. 39-E).
9. Insert inner pillow.
10. Blindstitch 4th side to boxing, turning raw edges inside (see fig. 39-F).

(Continued on next page)

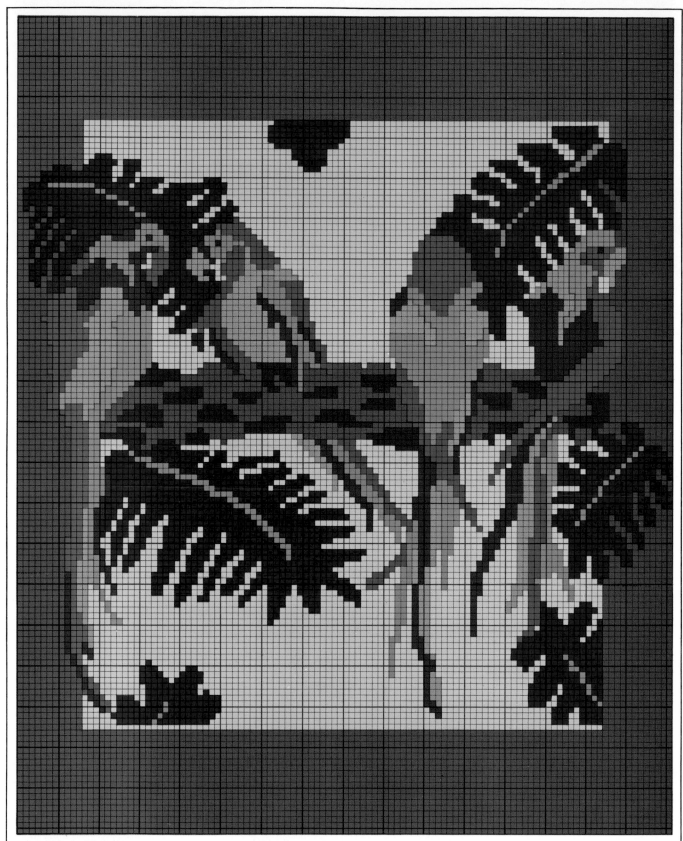

STITCH GUIDE

Basketweave
Mosaic (p. 22)

CANVAS

#7 rug-type
21 by 23-inch piece

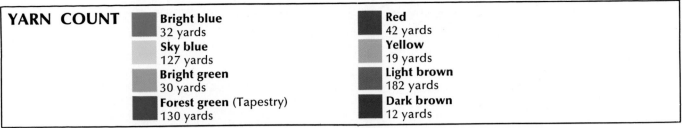

Bright blue 32 yards	**Red** 42 yards
Sky blue 127 yards	**Yellow** 19 yards
Bright green 30 yards	**Light brown** 182 yards
Forest green (Tapestry) 130 yards	**Dark brown** 12 yards

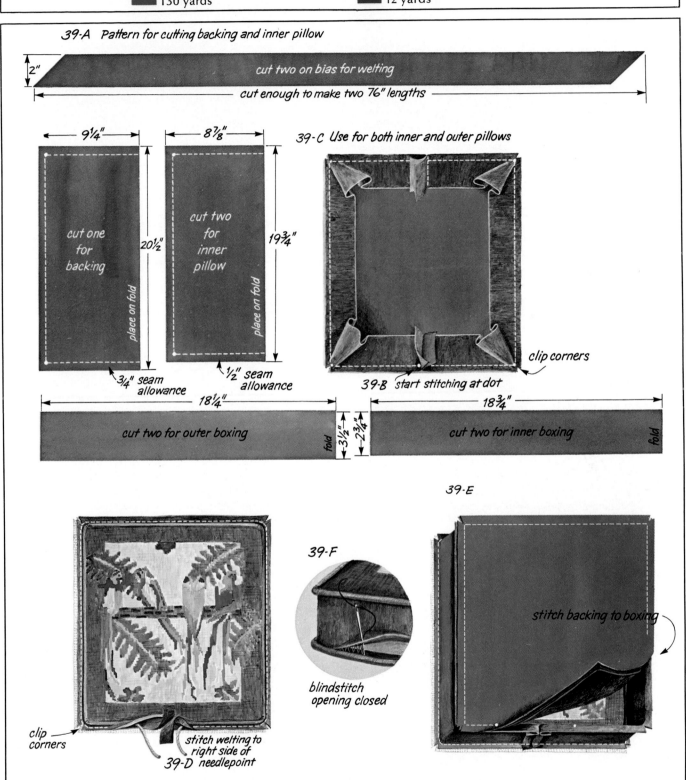

39-A Pattern for cutting backing and inner pillow

2"

cut two on bias for welting

cut enough to make two 76" lengths

9¼"

8⅞"

39-C Use for both inner and outer pillows

cut one for backing

cut two for inner pillow

20½"

19¾"

place on fold

place on fold

¾" seam allowance

½" seam allowance

39-B start stitching at dot

clip corners

18¼"

cut two for outer boxing

fold

3½" 2¾"

18¾"

cut two for inner boxing

fold

39-E

39-F

stitch backing to boxing

blindstitch opening closed

clip corners

stitch welting to right side of
39-D needlepoint

A Gaggle of Geese

Look closely at the pattern subtly stitched on these coasters and you'll see a gaggle of geese flying by. Backed with cork or wide-wale corduroy, these contemporary coasters won't slip or slide about on a tabletop. And they won't stick to the bottom of a wet glass.

To see how this clever design was adapted for the knife-edge pillow on page 42, just turn the page. By using a larger mesh canvas, adding birds to each row to fill a rectangular shape, and adopting a completely different color scheme, the designer has created an entirely new project from the same basic idea. With practice (and a little imagination), you'll soon be able to alter needlepoint designs and color schemes to fit your own needs.

Design: Lindsey Roscoe.

COASTERS

1. Enlarge design according to directions on page 12.
2. Bind edges of four 10-inch squares of 10/20 penelope canvas with masking tape. Draw outline of *each* square on brown paper and mark as shown on page 13.
3. Fold each square into quarters; unfold and mark center where both paper folds cross.
4. Cut a 4½-inch square of cardboard to form a pattern for coaster (save this pattern to use when finishing).
5. Lay pattern on unfolded canvas squares, with corners of pattern at fold lines (see fig. 41-A).
6. Draw around pattern with a gray indelible marker.
7. Work directly from graph, using it as a color guide.
8. Stitch central bird in basketweave or continental stitch, using 1 full thread of Persian yarn in a #18 tapestry needle.
9. From central bird, work out in all directions until you have completed all birds.
10. Stitch border last, using basketweave stitch with 1 full thread of Persian yarn.
11. Block according to directions on page 29.

FINISHING TECHNIQUES

You'll need: 12-inch square of backing fabric such as wide-wale corduroy cut on straight grain into four 6-inch squares; clear nylon thread and sewing needle. (Or use felt or ⅛-inch cork cut to exact size for each coaster and attach it to needlepoint with white glue.)

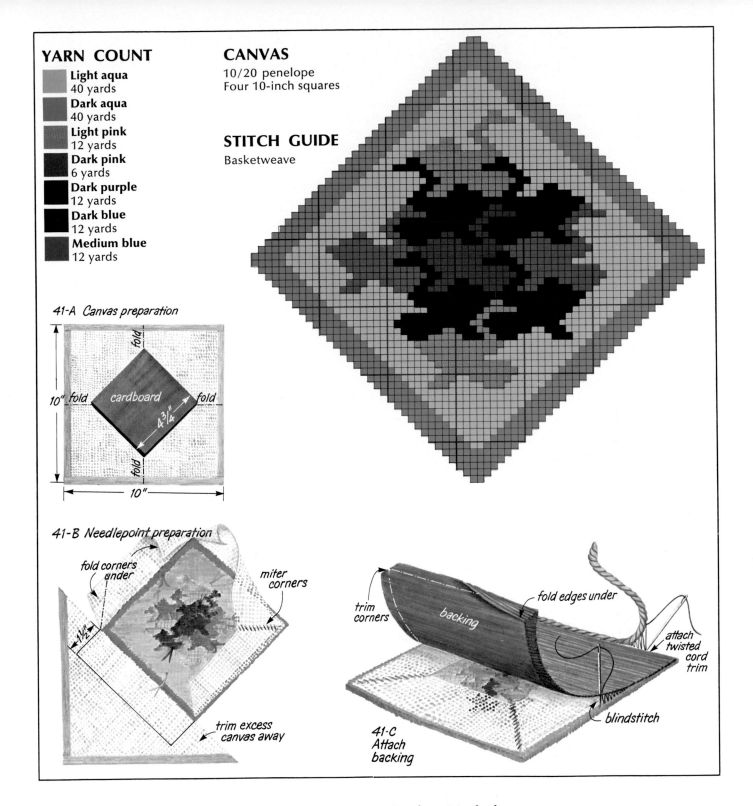

YARN COUNT

Light aqua
40 yards

Dark aqua
40 yards

Light pink
12 yards

Dark pink
6 yards

Dark purple
12 yards

Dark blue
12 yards

Medium blue
12 yards

CANVAS

10/20 penelope
Four 10-inch squares

STITCH GUIDE

Basketweave

41-A Canvas preparation

10"
10"
fold
fold
fold
fold
cardboard
4³/₄"

41-B Needlepoint preparation

fold corners under
miter corners
1½"
trim excess canvas away

trim corners
backing
fold edges under
attach twisted cord trim
blindstitch

41·C Attach backing

Coaster

1. After blocking, machine stitch 2 rows around edges of needlepoint to prevent canvas threads from raveling.
2. Trim canvas and miter corners as in figure 41-B.
3. Trim corners off backing fabric.
4. Turn edges of backing under and blindstitch (see fig. 41-C) along needlepointed edges.
5. If you like, trim with twisted cord (see page 31) or single crochet chain.

Project Variations

• Make a pincushion — stitch one 4-inch square as for a coaster, but finish according to directions on page 36.

• For a patchwork pillow, piece together several 4-inch "geese" squares with squares of fabric or plain needlepoint.

• Turn one coaster design into a box pillow by adding birds all around until it is the desired size.

(Continued on next page)

Gaggle of Geese Pillow

. . . Gaggle of Geese (cont'd.)

KNIFE-EDGE PILLOW

1. Enlarge design on facing page according to directions on page 12.

2. Bind edges of a 16¾ by 22-inch piece of #7 (rug-type) canvas with masking tape. Draw outline of canvas on brown paper and mark as shown on page 13.

3. With a gray indelible marker, draw a 12¾ by 18-inch rectangle on canvas, leaving a 2-inch border all around.

4. Using graph, draw birds onto canvas with indelible marker by counting squares on graph and matching squares with canvas threads. Because birds are in rows, it is best to work from top to bottom if you are right-handed; from bottom to top if you are left-handed.

5. With 6 strands of Persian yarn (1 full thread, doubled) in a #16 tapestry needle, work entire piece in basket-weave stitch.

6. Block according to directions on page 29.

FINISHING TECHNIQUES

You'll need: 16¾ by 22-inch piece of nubby woven fabric or velveteen for backing; matching thread; polyester batting for stuffing; ½ yard of 45-inch-wide muslin; clear nylon thread and sewing needle.

Inner Pillow

1. Cut 2 pieces of muslin, *each* 13½ by 19 inches.

2. Pin pieces together and machine stitch ½ inch from raw edge on all sides, leaving a 6-inch opening unstitched.

3. Turn right side out and stuff inner pillow with polyester batting until plump and firm.

4. Push polyester away from raw edge and secure with pins (see fig. 43-A).

5. Turn raw edges under ½ inch and machine stitch closed (see fig. 43-A).

6. Remove pins and rearrange stuffing to fill pillow evenly from top to bottom.

Outer Pillow Cover

1. After blocking, machine stitch 2 rows through canvas around edges of needlepointed area; remove binding.

2. Pin needlepoint to backing, right sides together.

3. Machine stitch (between last 2 rows of needlepoint stitches) around 3 sides of cover and 1½ inches in on *each* end of 4th side.

4. Trim seam allowance to ½ inch all around.

5. Turn pillow cover right side out.

6. Insert inner pillow and blindstitch (see page 39, fig. 39-F) last edge closed by hand.

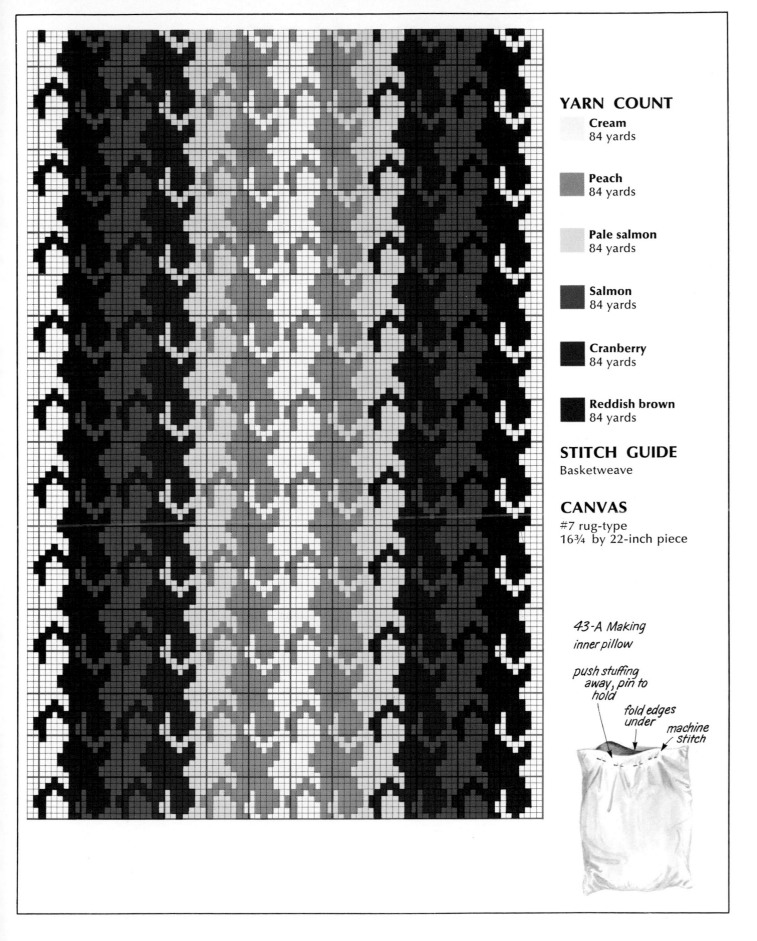

YARN COUNT

Cream
84 yards

Peach
84 yards

Pale salmon
84 yards

Salmon
84 yards

Cranberry
84 yards

Reddish brown
84 yards

STITCH GUIDE
Basketweave

CANVAS
#7 rug-type
16¾ by 22-inch piece

43-A Making
inner pillow

push stuffing
away, pin to
hold

fold edges
under

machine
stitch

Victorian House

YARN COUNT

☐	**White** 30 yards
	Light camel 40 yards
	Dark camel 20 yards
	Dark gray blue 30 yards
	Light gray blue 50 yards
	Dark olive green 20 yards
	Burnt sienna 30 yards
	Pale yellow 5 yards
	Pale yellow (Embroidery floss) 3 skeins

CANVAS

#13 mono
14 by 16-inch piece

A nostalgic reminder of the Victorian era, this handsome needlepoint picture will grace any room in which it hangs. The designer, inspired by the building's crisp architectural lines, has accurately duplicated the elegance of a charming San Francisco structure.

The nature of the design, with its straight lines and distinctive coloration, lends itself well to a picture format, but it could work equally well as a pillow or a photo album cover. It is shown here professionally framed, a light linen mat and pale gold frame enhancing the finished piece.

A variety of decorative stitches skillfully worked gives this needlepoint project unique depth and luster. A deft hand is required to produce the collection of stitches included in this design; practice until you have mastered them — then "build" a Victorian house of your own.

Design: Peter Ashe and Vera Kloppenburg.

1. Bind edges of a 14 by 16-inch piece of #13 mono canvas with masking tape.
2. With a gray indelible marker, draw outline of 10 by 12-inch design, leaving a 2-inch border all around.
3. Work directly from graph; draw lines on canvas to distinguish areas where decorative stitches will be used.
4. Following stitch guide, work all decorative stitches with a #20 tapestry needle. All decorative stitches listed there are worked with 2 strands from a thread of Persian yarn. Example: Upright Gobelin—3 means: Use 3 strands of yarn.
5. Next, work each of the "glass windows," using 6 strands of embroidery floss. These small rectangular shapes will give you centers from which other stitches will radiate.
6. Complete basketweave areas, including sky blue background, using 2 strands from a thread of Persian yarn.

FINISHING TECHNIQUES

If you plan to have this piece framed, it needn't be blocked. A professional framer will pull the needlepoint into alignment over a stiff backing that is padded with polyester batting to give a soft, cushiony feel to the finished piece.

If you've done a fair amount of framing, you might want to frame the needlepoint yourself.

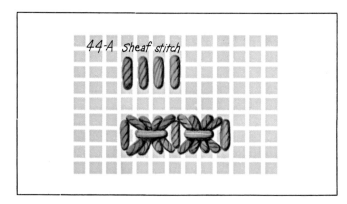

44-A Sheaf stitch

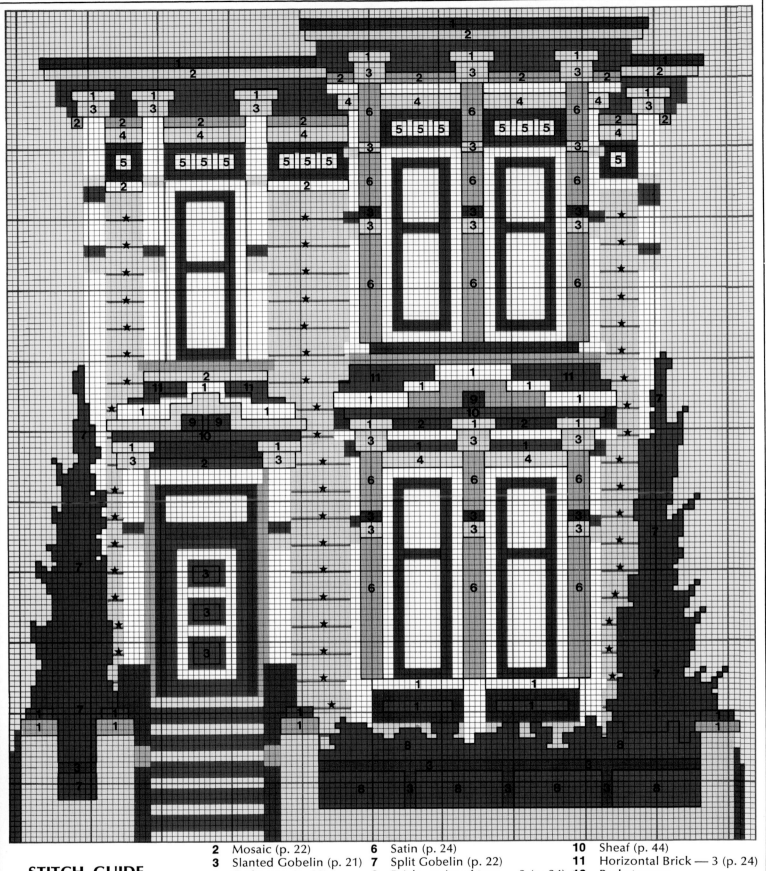

STITCH GUIDE

1 Upright Gobelin — 3 (p. 21)	**2** Mosaic (p. 22)	**6** Satin (p. 24)
	3 Slanted Gobelin (p. 21)	**7** Split Gobelin (p. 22)
	4 Cashmere (p. 22)	**8** Brick—pairs of two — 3 (p. 24)
	5 Scotch (p. 23)	**9** Double Leviathan (p. 21)

10 Sheaf (p. 44)	
11 Horizontal Brick — 3 (p. 24)	
12 Basketweave	
★ Backstitch — 1 (p. 21)	

Bear Hugs

It looks as though this lumbering fellow will have no lunch today — his shimmering catch seems ready to escape. But you can capture the scene forever in needlepoint on this shaped box pillow.

The entire piece is done in basketweave stitch with Persian wool; perle cotton is used for the fish so that it looks freshly snatched from a cool mountain stream. Stitching with perle cotton and wool together in the needle may be difficult for the beginner (they tend to tangle), but with practice the work should go smoothly.

Design: Jan Magdaleno.

1. Enlarge design according to directions on page 12.
2. Bind edges of a 16-inch square of #10 mono canvas with masking tape. Draw outline of canvas on brown paper and mark as shown on page 13.
3. Trace enlarged design onto canvas with gray indelible marker; keep a 2-inch border all around. Save pattern.

4. With 1 strand from a thread of Persian yarn and 1 strand of perle cotton in a #18 tapestry needle, work fish in basketweave stitch.
5. Stitch bear in basketweave with 1 full thread of Persian yarn.
6. Block according to directions on page 29.

FINISHING TECHNIQUES

You'll need: 16-inch square of backing fabric such as brown wide-wale corduroy or velveteen; matching thread; 3½ by 41-inch length of fabric for boxing; 88 inches of ¼-inch-diameter cord for welting; clear nylon thread and sewing needle; polyester batting for stuffing; 20 inches of 45-inch-wide muslin for inner pillow.

Finish as for box pillow on page 37, using enlarged drawing as a pattern for cutting out backing, and adding a ¾-inch seam allowance all around.

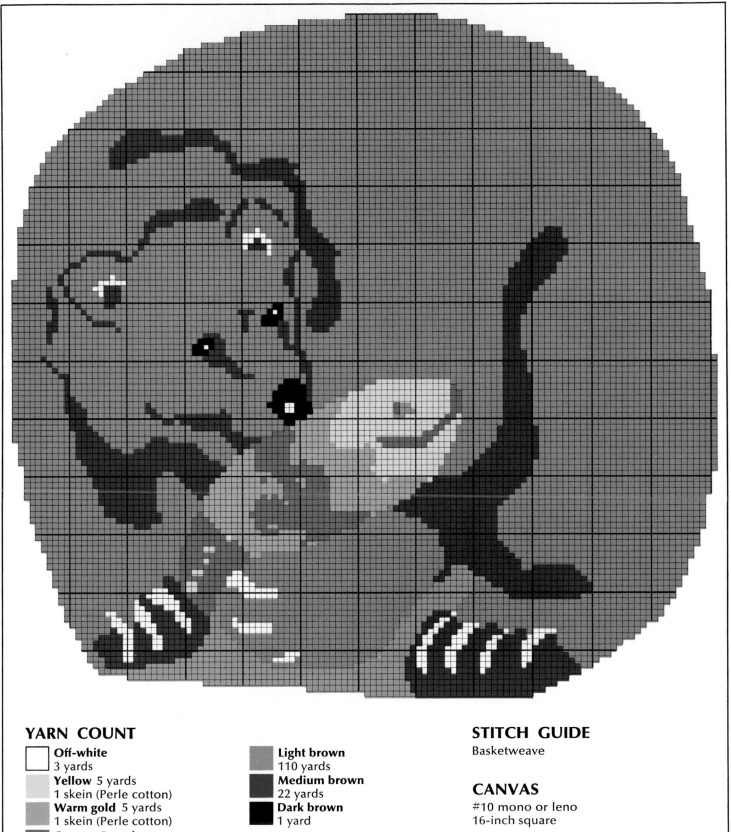

YARN COUNT

Off-white
3 yards

Yellow 5 yards
1 skein (Perle cotton)

Warm gold 5 yards
1 skein (Perle cotton)

Orange 5 yards
1 skein (Perle cotton)

Medium blue
7 yards

Light brown
110 yards

Medium brown
22 yards

Dark brown
1 yard

STITCH GUIDE

Basketweave

CANVAS

#10 mono or leno
16-inch square

Hopi Indian Duo

The use of sophisticated designs and natural dyes distinguished the Hopi Indians (or "Peaceful Ones") as skilled artisans of the early Southwest. Prompted by the Hopis' use of rich earth tones and symbolic motifs, our designer has re-created a bit of Indian heritage in this clutch and eyeglass case ensemble.

The smart clutch, with its freeform adaptation of a Hopi pottery design, is lined in blue gray faille and is the perfect accompaniment to today's ethnic and classic looks.

The more intricately detailed coordinated eyeglass case is a combination of stylized patterns done on petit point canvas. Tawa, the Sun God, radiates from one corner, accented by a typical bear print motif. The small, round symbol indicates clouds of rain in Hopi art language; a touch of Hopi-inspired pottery design trims the corner opposite Tawa.

Design: Jane Aurich.

EYEGLASS CASE

1. Bind edges of an 11-inch square of #18 mono canvas with masking tape. Draw outline of canvas on brown paper and mark as shown on page 13.
2. With gray indelible marker, draw a 6½ by 6¾-inch rectangle centered on canvas, leaving a 2-inch border all around.
3. Roughly trace design onto canvas with indelible marker; then work directly from graph.
4. First stitch design areas (other than black) in basketweave stitch with 1 strand from a thread of Persian yarn in a #20 tapestry needle.
5. Stitch black areas last, using 1 strand of Persian yarn.

6. Block according to directions on page 29.

CLUTCH

1. Enlarge design according to directions on page 12.
2. Bind edges of a 14½ by 26-inch piece of #12 mono canvas with masking tape. Draw outline of canvas on brown paper and mark as shown on page 13.
3. Trace enlarged design onto canvas with gray indelible marker, leaving a 2-inch border all around. Keep pattern for use in finishing.
4. First work design areas (other than black) in basketweave stitch with 2 strands from a thread of Persian yarn in a #18 tapestry needle. You can also begin stitching background, switching from design areas to background for a change of pace; use basketweave and 2 strands of Persian yarn.
5. Stitch black areas last, also in basketweave stitch with 2 strands of Persian yarn.
6. Block according to directions on page 29.

FINISHING TECHNIQUES

You'll need: Eyeglass Case—11-inch square of steel gray faille for lining; matching thread; clear nylon thread and sewing needle; 18½ inches twisted cord trim (see page 31). **Clutch**—11½ by 23-inch piece of steel gray faille for lining; matching thread; clear nylon thread and sewing needle; 9½ by 21-inch piece of interlining.

Eyeglass Case

Finish according to directions on page 62.

(Continued on page 52)

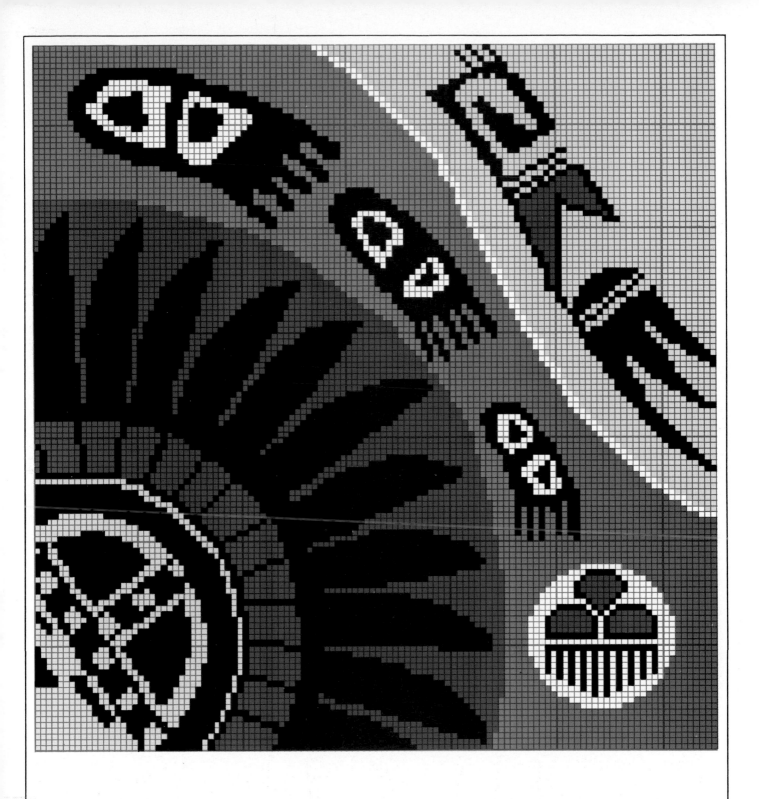

YARN COUNT

Honey beige 5 yards		**Dark pottery red** 4 yards
White 2 yards		**Black** 6½ yards
Dark steel gray 4½ yards		

STITCH GUIDE

Basketweave

CANVAS

#18 mono
11-inch square

STITCH GUIDE
Basketweave

CANVAS
#12 mono
14½ by 26 inch piece

YARN COUNT

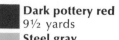

Light honey beige 28½ yards	Dark pottery red 9½ yards
Honey beige 18½ yards	Steel gray 56 yards
Earth brown 23 yards	Dark steel gray 35 yards
Light pottery red 3½ yards	Black 15½ yards

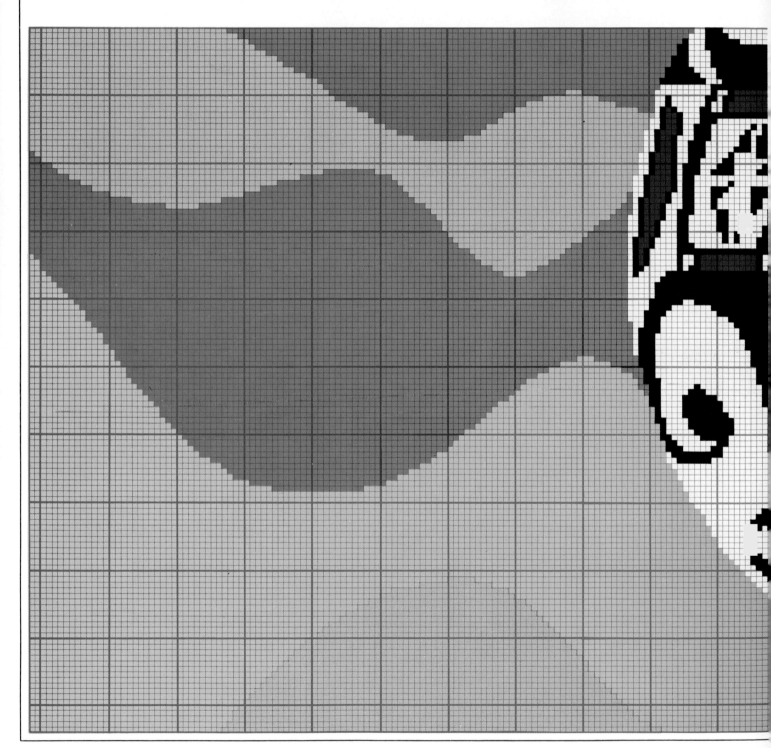

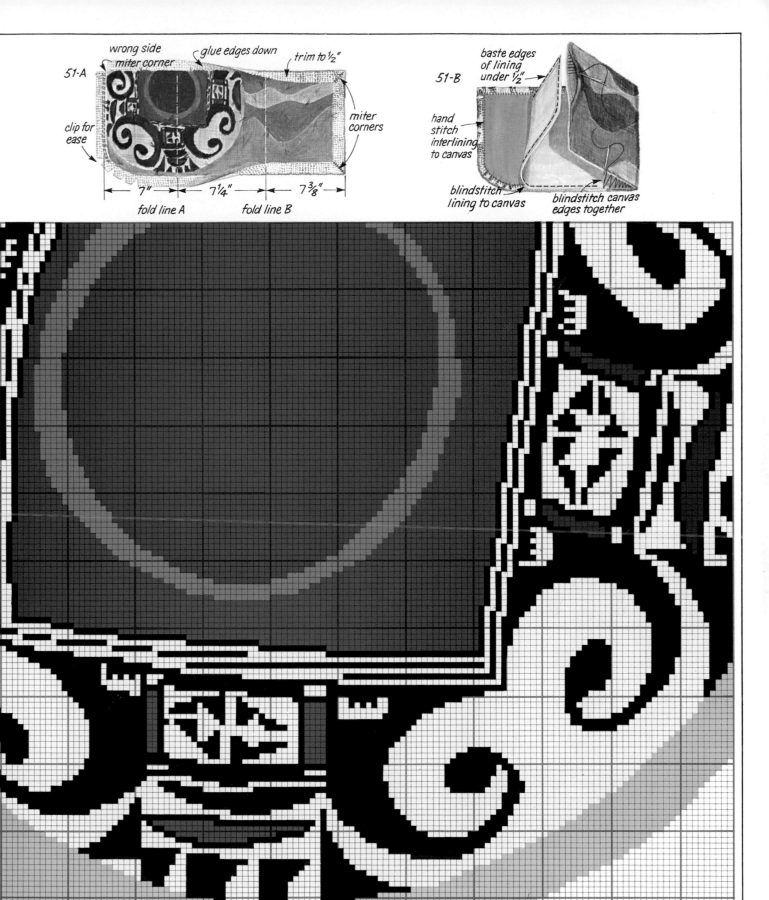

51-A

wrong side
miter corner

glue edges down

trim to ½"

clip for
ease

miter
corners

|← 7" →|← 7¼" →|← 7⅜" →|

fold line A

fold line B

51-B

baste edges
of lining
under ½"

hand
stitch
interling
to canvas

blindstitch
lining to canvas

blindstitch canvas
edges together

(Continued on next page)

Clutch

1. After blocking, machine stitch 2 rows through canvas edges of needlepointed areas to prevent canvas threads from raveling; remove binding and trim excess canvas to ½ inch all around.
2. Turn canvas edges under; then miter 3 remaining corners (see fig. 51-A).
3. Using enlarged drawing as a guide, cut interlining ½ inch smaller all around; then cut lining in same fashion, adding ½-inch seam allowance all around.

4. Center interlining on wrong side of canvas; a ½-inch edging of bare canvas will remain all around.
5. Handstitch interlining to bare canvas (see fig. 51-B).
6. Baste ½-inch seam allowance of lining under.
7. Lay wrong sides of needlepoint and lining together and baste.
8. Blindstitch lining to needlepoint (see fig. 51-B).
9. Fold piece along line B and stitch sides together with clear nylon thread, taking extra reinforcement stitches at corners.
10. Fold at line A and secure flap with snaps, if desired.

Cows in Clover

How else would you describe the charming pastoral picture on this welt-seamed, knife-edge pillow? Originally designed to be used on a ladder-back or rocking chair (as shown at left), this project can take on many other guises — toss it on your sofa for a touch of rustic simplicity or let it brighten your child's room.

This is a project that stitches up more quickly than you might expect, thanks partly to the fact that the diagonal cashmere stitch is used for the vibrant green background.

Design: Joanne and Robert Herzog.

1. Enlarge design according to directions on page 12.
2. Bind edges of an 18 by 20-inch piece of #7 (rug-type) canvas with masking tape. Draw outline of canvas on brown paper and mark as shown on page 13.
3. With a gray indelible marker, draw a 14 by 16-inch rectangle on canvas, leaving a 2-inch border all around.
4. Trace design onto canvas, or work directly from graph.
5. Using a #16 tapestry needle with 6 strands of Persian yarn (1 full thread, doubled), stitch all cows and birds in either basketweave or continental stitch.
6. Complete pillow by filling in green grass in diagonal cashmere stitch (page 22) with 6 strands of Persian yarn.
7. Block according to directions on page 29.

FINISHING TECHNIQUES

You'll need: 15½ by 17½-inch piece of brown backing fabric such as imitation suede or velveteen; matching thread; 64 inches of ¼-inch-diameter cord for welting; four 7-inch ties (see page 31); clear nylon thread and sewing needle; polyester batting for stuffing; ½ yard of 36-inch-wide muslin for inner pillow.

Pillow Cover

1. After blocking, machine stitch 2 rows through canvas around needlepointed area to prevent canvas threads from raveling; remove binding.
2. Make welting and ties according to directions on pages 30–31.
3. Using ¾-inch seam allowances, finish as for knife-edge pillow on page 42, but stitch welting and corner ties into seam as directed on pages 30 and 31.

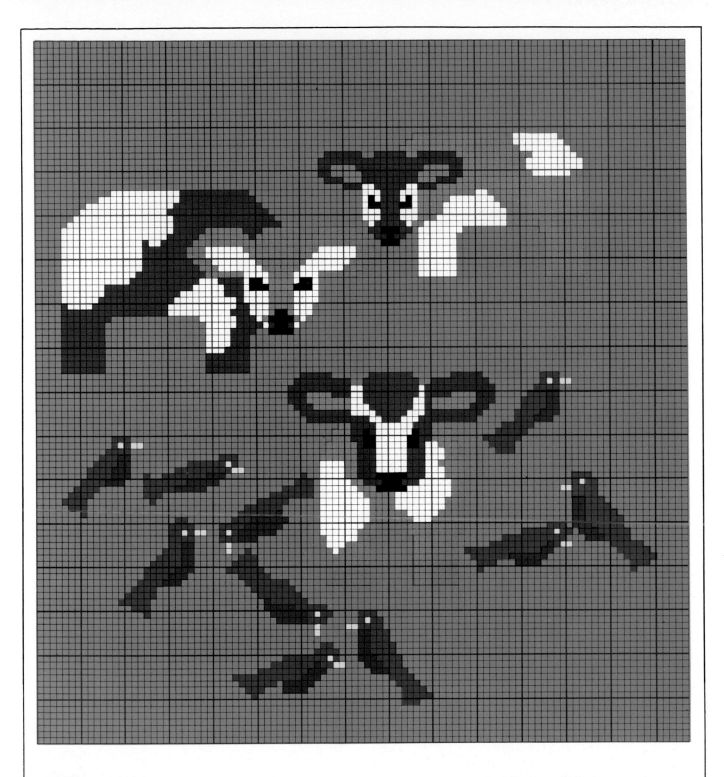

YARN COUNT

Light brown
18½ yards

Medium brown
21¼ yards

Dark brown
4 yards

Grass green
141 yards

White
22 yards

Yellow
2 yards

Red
7½ yards

Blue
18½ yards

STITCH GUIDE

Basketweave or Continental
Diagonal Cashmere (p. 22)

CANVAS

#7 rug-type
18 by 20-inch piece

Cereal Box Pillow

A wholesome dab of nostalgia, this unique box pillow may be just the right color spot to highlight a contemporary or traditional room.

The "Jewel T" symbol, adapted from an original logogram, has been interpreted by our designer in a soft, sculptured style.

The pillow face is worked in Gobelin, mosaic, and basketweave or continental stitch, with special attention given to the "mitered" corners of the white border design (see fig. 57-A). An accompanying band that becomes the sides of the box is done in a variety of decorative stitches.

Design: Sue Walther.

FRONT OF BOX

1. Enlarge design according to directions on page 12.
2. Bind edges of a 14¼ by 17¼ -inch piece of #12 mono or leno canvas with masking tape. Draw outline of canvas on brown paper and mark as shown on page 13.
3. Roughly trace cereal box design onto canvas with gray indelible marker; letters should be perfectly centered on canvas. Use both stitch graph and tracing to work design. (Note: Entire piece is worked with 1 full thread of Persian yarn in a #18 tapestry needle.)
4. Stitch white border on top half in Gobelin (see page 21) over 4 canvas threads, "mitering" corners as in figure 57-A, page 57.
5. Center JEWEL T within white border; stitch gold, then white lettering in continental.
6. Using basketweave or continental stitch, fill in gold-outlined area with red; then stitch blue area surrounding JEWEL T.
7. Center and work TOASTED THICK in mosaic stitch (see page 22).
8. Using continental stitch, center and outline CORNFLAKES in blue; fill in with red continental stitch.
9. Stitch OVEN FRESH, TRIPLE-SEALED, READY TO SERVE in white half cross stitch.
10. Outline blue area (X's) at bottom in mosaic stitch; then fill in this area in blue basketweave or continental.
11. Stitch white background area in basketweave or continental stitch.

(Continued on page 57)

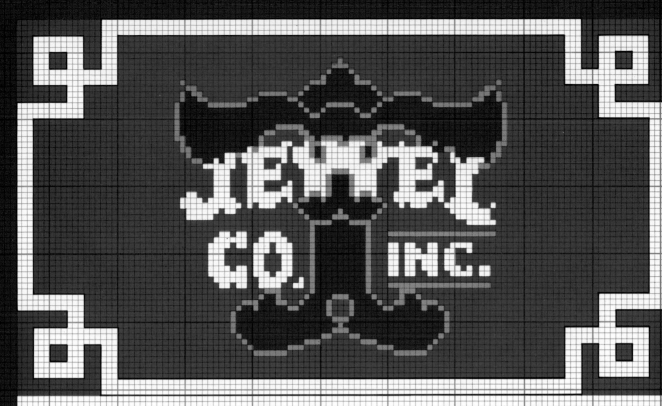

TOASTED·THICK
CORN FLAKES

OVEN FRESH
TRIPLE~SEALED
READY TO SERVE

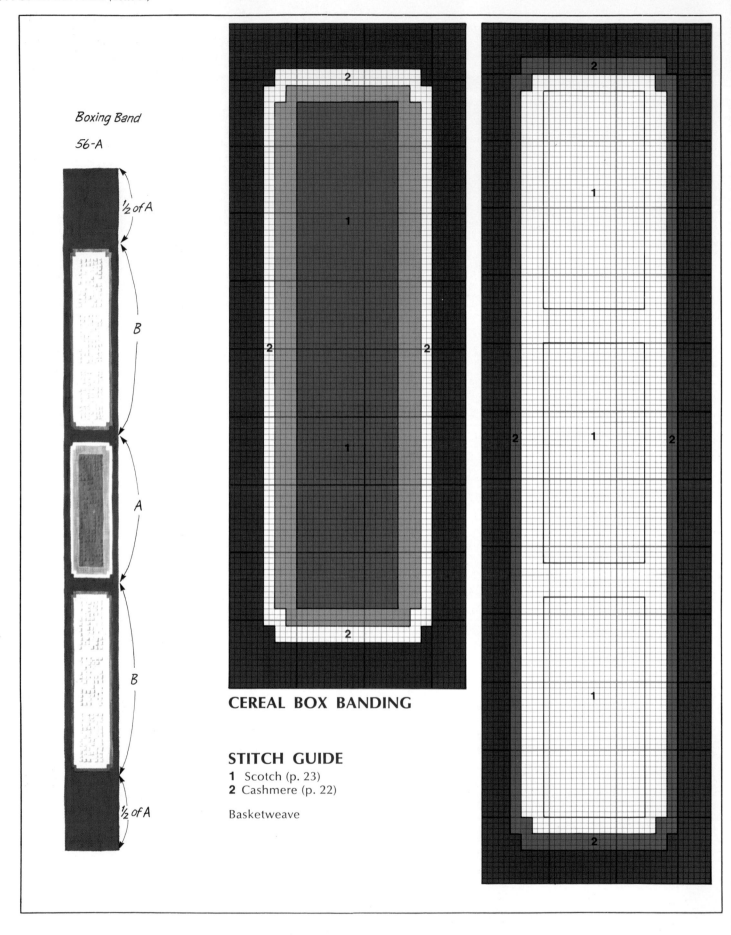

Boxing Band

56-A

½ of A

B

A

B

½ of A

CEREAL BOX BANDING

STITCH GUIDE
1 Scotch (p. 23)
2 Cashmere (p. 22)

Basketweave

12. Work red border in basketweave or continental. (Red border is 6 stitches wide; 3 of these 6 rows are used in seam allowance when finishing pillow.)
13. Block according to directions on page 29.

SIDES OF BOX

Note: Graph for band has been broken down into 2 main sections — 1 end (section "A") and 1 side (section "B"). "A" and "B" are pieced together as shown in figure 56-A to produce a continuous band that forms the sides of cereal box.

1. Bind edges of a 7½ by 48-inch piece of #12 mono or leno canvas with masking tape.
2. Draw outline of 3½ by 44-inch band on canvas with gray indelible marker, leaving a 2-inch border all around. Draw outline of canvas on brown paper and mark as shown on page 13. Also draw lines on canvas between "sections" to use as a guide when you stitch. *Remember:* By counting squares on graph you can determine number of stitches in any given area.

3. Starting at either end, work a red section (½ size of section "A") in basketweave stitch.
4. Continue by stitching "B," "A," "B," and finally second red section "A" as in step 3.
5. Block according to directions on page 29.

FINISHING TECHNIQUES

You'll need: 11½ by 14½ inches red velveteen for backing; matching thread; clear nylon thread and sewing needle; polyester batting; ½ yard of 36-inch-wide muslin.

Cereal Box

1. After blocking, machine stitch 2 rows through canvas around needlepointed areas of front and band of pillow to prevent canvas threads from raveling; remove binding and trim excess canvas to ¾ inch all around.
2. Following directions for making a box pillow on page 37, omit welting and use needlepointed band for boxing. Join seams of boxing and pillow face at a point 3 stitched rows in from both edges of stitching (see fig. 57-B).

YARN COUNT

■ **White**
80 yards

■ **Red**
64 yards

■ **Gold**
10 yards

■ **Blue**
70 yards

STITCH GUIDE

Basketweave
Scotch (p. 23)
Straight Gobelin (p. 21)
Mosaic (p. 22)
Cashmere (p. 22)

CANVAS

#12 mono or leno
14¼ by 17¼ -inch piece

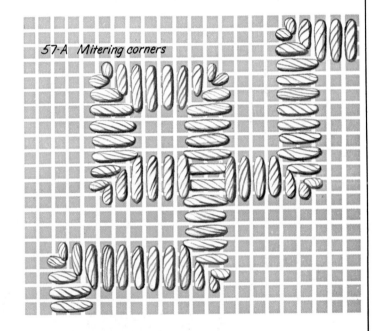

57-A   Mitering corners

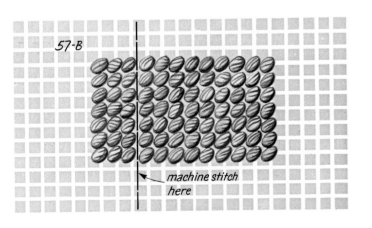

57-B

machine stitch here

1903 Sunset Cover

L. Maynard Dixon painted the original of this classic *Sunset Magazine* cover for the May 1903 issue. We've reproduced it as a needlepoint poster, professionally framed with a simple wooden border suggesting the Old West.

(Continued on page 60)

The richly textured look of the background is achieved by the combining of blue, rust, and off-white Persian yarn strands into thread groups. Preparing the thread groups is a time-consuming process that is best done before you begin to stitch; this way your work will go easily. A needle-threader (see fig. 60-A, page 60) is a useful tool for combining various strands of yarn.

You separate the threads of the penelope canvas to work the Indian's face in petit point stitches. Otherwise, the entire piece is worked in gros point .

A project for the advanced needlepointer, our *Sunset* cover offers an interesting means to a textural end by combining gros point and petit point stitching to enhance the pattern's fine details.

Design adaptation: Diane Tapscott.

1. Enlarge design according to directions on page 12.
2. Bind edges of a 16¼ by 22-inch piece of 10/20 penelope canvas with masking tape.
3. Center design and roughly trace onto canvas with gray indelible marker.
4. Following graph on this page, stitch Indian's face in petit point (either basketweave or continental), using 1 strand from a thread of Persian yarn in a #20 tapestry needle. (Follow suggestions on page 6 for separating canvas threads and working petit point on 10/20 penelope canvas.)

5. Using graph as a guide, work remainder of Indian in basketweave stitch, using 1 full thread of Persian yarn in a #18 tapestry needle.
6. Stitch lettering in basketweave with 1 full thread of Persian yarn.
7. Using basketweave, stitch background as indicated on graph, using thread groups represented by symbols that outline areas of each group:
ヽ 2 strands off-white/1 strand rust
× 2 strands red/1 strand royal blue
● 1 strand off-white/1 strand royal blue/1 strand rust
+ 2 strands royal blue/1 strand white
8. Stitch blue border in basketweave, using 1 full thread of Persian yarn. To complete border, add 7 rows of blue above 2 rows of ●'s at top of graph and 13 rows of blue below 2 rows of ●'s at bottom of graph.

FINISHING TECHNIQUES

See finishing instructions for "Victorian House," page 44. If you plan to have this piece professionally framed, it needn't be blocked.

YARN COUNT

- ■ **Dark blue black** 82½ yards
- ■ **Royal blue** 104½ yards
- ■ **Red** 19¼ yards
- ■ **Rust** 38½ yards
- **Off-white** 44 yards
- □ **White** 6 yards

SYMBOLS — 1903 SUNSET COVER

ヽ 2 strands off-white/1 strand rust
× 2 strands red/1 strand royal blue
● 1 strand off-white/1 strand royal blue/1 strand rust
+ 2 strands royal blue/1 strand rust

STITCH GUIDE

Basketweave (petit point and gros point)

CANVAS

10/20 penelope
16¼ by 22-inch piece

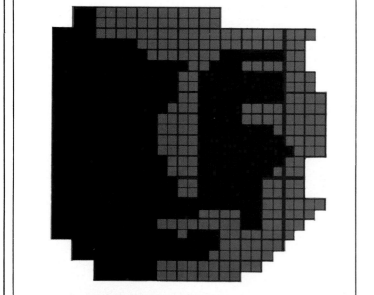

DETAIL—INDIAN'S FACE

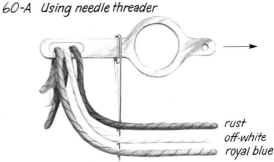

60-A Using needle threader

rust
off-white
royal blue

Positively Poppies

Smashing red poppies elegantly stitched against a black background form the basis for a sophisticated trio of accessories — saddlebag tote, checkbook cover, and eyeglass case — to accent your wardrobe.

Clusters of shiny black beads scattered about the center of the large poppy, plus bamboo-ring handles and nubby woven black fabric back give the tote a chic, snappy style.

Checks and stripes neatly contrast with and complement the solid black background of the tote. The eyeglass case and checkbook cover work up quickly in large decorative stitches — each is an attractive offshoot of the more challenging tote bag.

Design: Marinda Brown.

EYEGLASS CASE

1. Enlarge design according to directions on page 12.
2. Bind edges of an 11-inch square of #12 mono or leno canvas with masking tape. Draw outline of canvas on brown paper and mark as shown on page 13.
3. With gray indelible marker, draw a 7-inch square on canvas, leaving a 2-inch border all around.
4. To stitch, work directly from graph. Use 1 full thread of tapestry wool (6 strands) in a #18 tapestry needle to stitch center of poppy in basketweave.

5. With 1 full thread of tapestry wool, stitch remainder of poppy, using basketweave.
6. Stitch white stripes in satin stitch (see page 24) over 5 vertical threads, with backstitch (see page 21) to separate rows; use 2 strands from a thread of Persian yarn.
7. Work black stripes in kalem stitch (see page 25), using 2 strands of Persian yarn.
8. Block according to directions on page 29.

CHECKBOOK COVER

1. Repeat steps 1–5 as for eyeglass case.
2. Using 2 strands from a thread of Persian yarn, work white squares in Scotch stitch. (Note: For steps 2 and 3, you may use any of the Scotch stitch variations illustrated on pages 23 and 24.)
3. Finish checkerboard pattern, using 2 strands of black Persian yarn as in step 2.
4. Block according to directions on page 29.

SADDLEBAG TOTE

1. Enlarge design according to directions on page 12.

(Continued on next page)

POPPY EYEGLASS CASE

STITCH GUIDE

Backstitch (p. 21)
Straight Gobelin (p. 21)
Kalem (p. 25)

CANVAS

#12 mono or leno
11-inch square

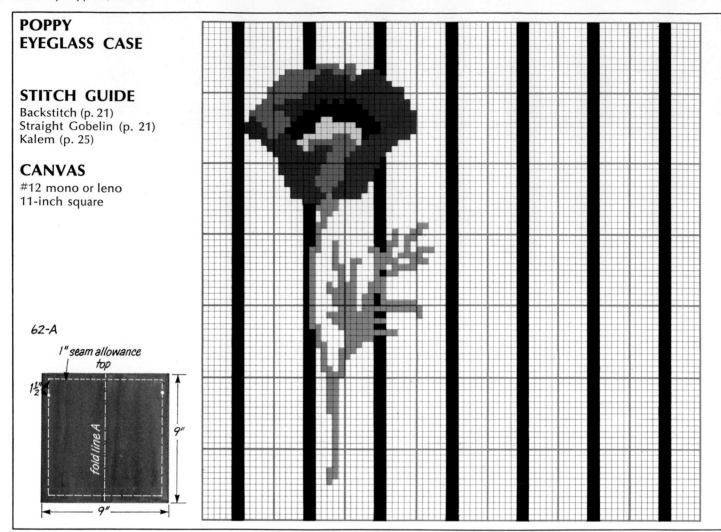

62-A

1" seam allowance top

1½"

fold line A

9"

9"

2. Bind edges of a 19 by 20-inch piece of #12 mono or leno canvas with masking tape. Draw outline of canvas on brown paper and mark as shown on page 13.

3. Use enlarged design as pattern, centering it on canvas and tracing outline with gray indelible marker; save pattern for use in finishing.

4. Draw poppy on canvas with indelible marker, or work directly from graph. It will be helpful to color in background with black acrylic paint; this will prevent any canvas from peeking through to surface of finished piece. (Read page 14 for instructions on painting canvas.)

5. For center of poppy, work spider web stitch (see fig. 64-A) with 2 strands of Persian yarn, using a #20 tapestry needle.

6. Complete poppy with 1 full thread of tapestry wool in a #18 tapestry needle, using basketweave stitch.

7. Work background in basketweave stitch, using 2 strands from a thread of Persian yarn.

8. String 3 to 5 beads at a time on black embroidery floss and, with long stitches, secure randomly around center of poppy (fig. 64-B).

9. Block according to directions on page 29.

FINISHING TECHNIQUES

You'll need: Eyeglass Case—9-inch square of lining fabric such as black velveteen; matching thread; white glue; clear nylon thread and sewing needle; 20 inches twisted cord trim (see page 31). **Checkbook Cover**—8 by 22-inch piece of lining fabric such as black velveteen; matching thread; sewing needle and clear nylon thread. **Totebag**—½ yard of 36-inch-wide black cotton for lining; ½ yard of 36-inch-wide nubby black fabric; thread; two 9-inch bamboo-ring handles.

Eyeglass Case

1. After blocking, machine stitch 2 rows through canvas around needlepointed edges to prevent canvas threads from raveling; remove binding. Trim excess canvas to 1 inch all around.

2. Pin lining to needlepoint, right sides together.

3. Machine stitch across top and 1½ inches down *each* side (see fig. 62-A).

4. Continue by following steps 4–12 for finishing scissors case on page 36.

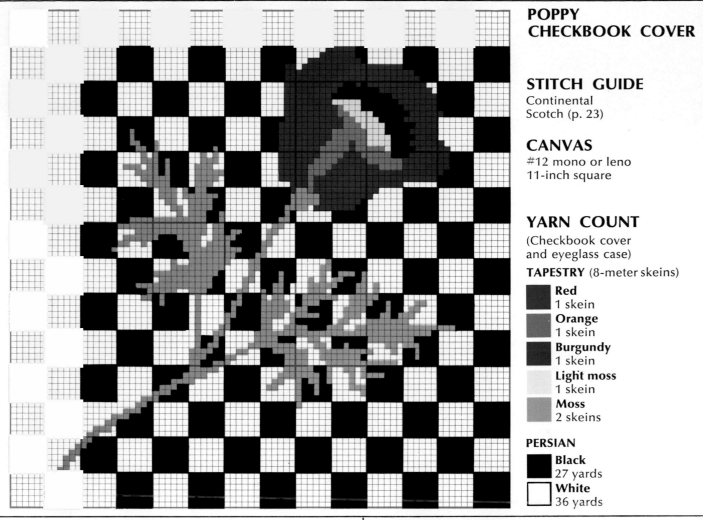

STITCH GUIDE
Continental
Scotch (p. 23)

CANVAS
#12 mono or leno
11-inch square

YARN COUNT
(Checkbook cover
and eyeglass case)

TAPESTRY (8-meter skeins)

Red
1 skein

Orange
1 skein

Burgundy
1 skein

Light moss
1 skein

Moss
2 skeins

PERSIAN

Black
27 yards

White
36 yards

Checkbook Cover

1. After blocking, machine stitch 2 rows through canvas around edges of needlepointed area to prevent canvas threads from raveling; remove binding. Trim excess canvas to ½ inch all around.

2. Cut and mark lining fabric on wrong side, according to layout 63-A. Baste fold lines and seamlines in contrasting thread.

3. Fold along lines marked A, so that right sides of fabric meet (fig. 63-B). Press lightly.

4. Fold along lines marked B so that wrong sides of fabric meet. Press lightly. You now have 2 pockets.

5. Pin needlepoint to lining, right sides together; machine stitch around 3 sides, to dots on side 4.

6. Turn right side out and blindstitch (see page 39, fig. 39-F) opening closed.

Totebag

1. After blocking, machine stitch 2 rows through canvas around needlepointed area to prevent canvas threads from raveling; remove binding. Trim seam to ⅝ inch.

(Continued on page 66)

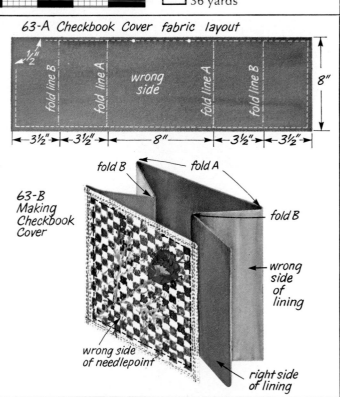

63-A Checkbook Cover fabric layout

fold line B · fold line A · wrong side · fold line A · fold line B

½"

8"

3½" · 3½" · 8" · 3½" · 3½"

63-B Making Checkbook Cover

fold B · fold A · fold B

wrong side of lining

wrong side of needlepoint

right side of lining

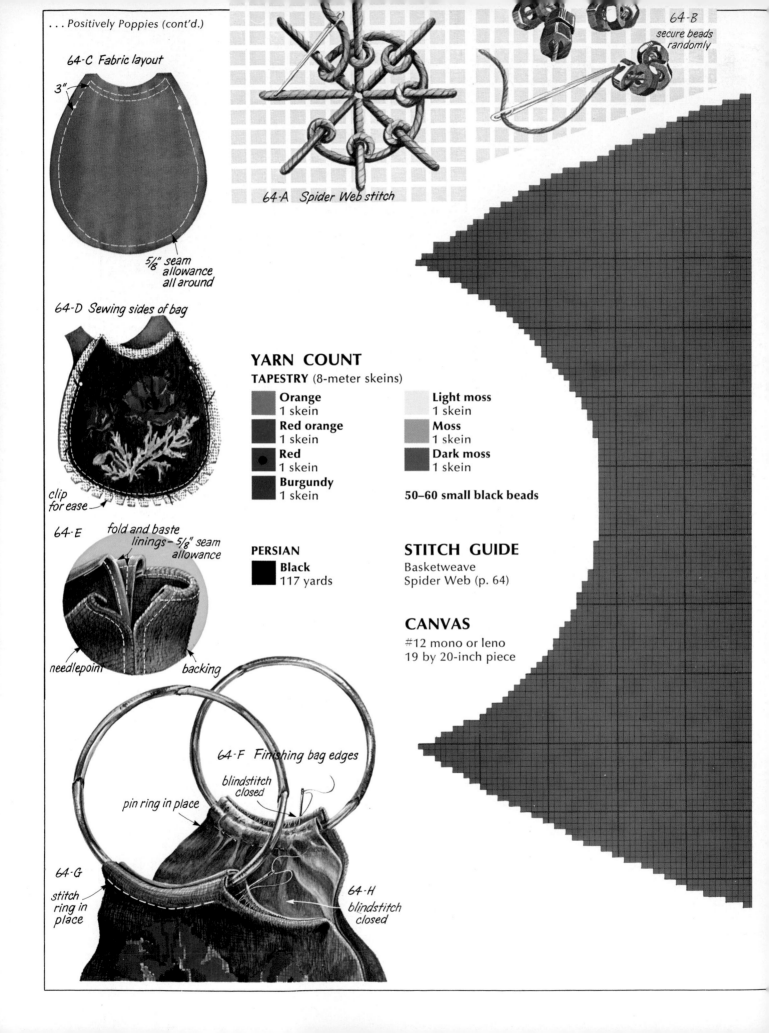

64-C Fabric layout

3"

5/8" seam allowance all around

64-A Spider Web stitch

64-B secure beads randomly

64-D Sewing sides of bag

clip for ease

64-E

fold and baste linings—5/8" seam allowance

needlepoint

backing

YARN COUNT
TAPESTRY (8-meter skeins)

Orange 1 skein

Red orange 1 skein

Red 1 skein

Burgundy 1 skein

Light moss 1 skein

Moss 1 skein

Dark moss 1 skein

50–60 small black beads

PERSIAN

Black 117 yards

STITCH GUIDE
Basketweave
Spider Web (p. 64)

CANVAS
#12 mono or leno
19 by 20-inch piece

64-F Finishing bag edges

blindstitch closed

pin ring in place

64-G
stitch ring in place

64-H
blindstitch closed

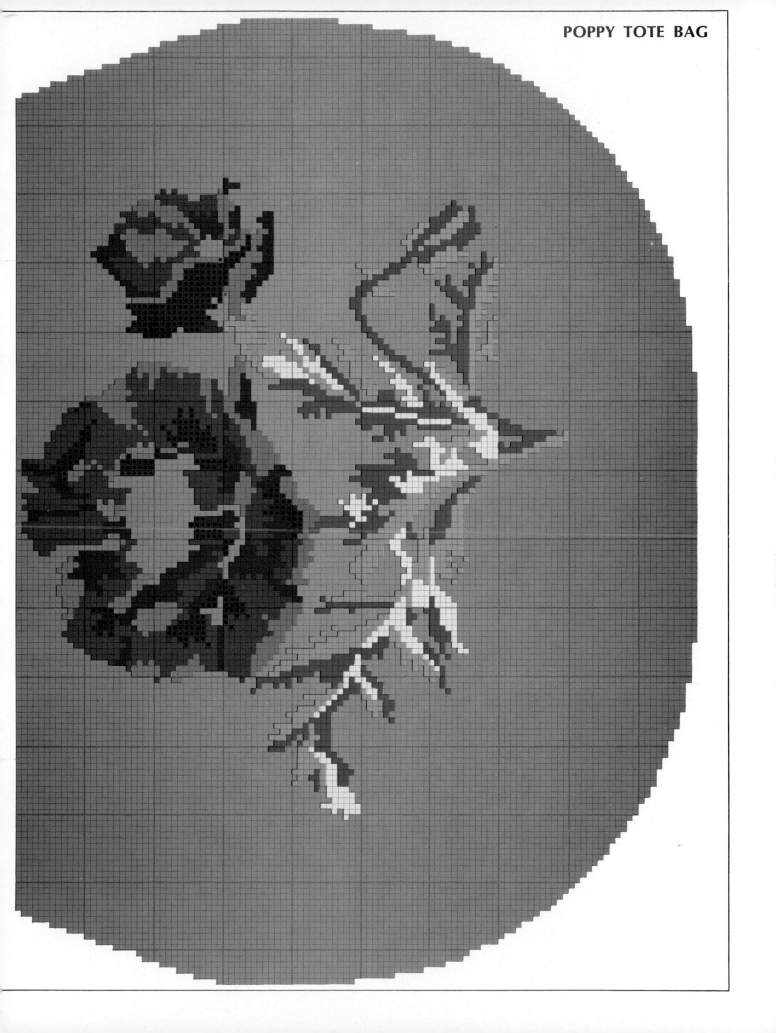

2. Using pattern from enlarged design, cut backing for bag, adding 5/8 inch all around for seam allowance.

3. Pin needlepoint to backing, right sides together, and stitch from dot to dot between last 2 rows of needlepoint stitches as shown in figure 64-C.

4. Clip seam allowance curves where necessary to allow seam to lie flat when tote bag is turned right side out (fig. 64-D).

5. Turn bag right side out.

6. Cut 2 pieces of lining fabric, using pattern in step 2.

7. Pin right sides of lining together and stitch between notches, leaving top open.

8. Trim seam to 1/4 inch all around; clip curves where necessary.

9. Insert lining into bag.

10. Turn under unstitched edges of lining, needlepoint, and backing fabric; baste each separately (see fig. 64-E).

11. Insert 1 bamboo ring between lining and needlepoint along upper edge of bag. Pin to hold bamboo ring in place while you blindstitch lining and needlepoint together along top edge (fig. 64-F).

12. Remove pins and push bamboo ring up to top edge (fig. 64-G).

13. Handstitch just below bamboo ring with black thread to hold ring in place.

14. Blindstitch lining and needlepoint together from notch to bamboo ring, making certain that edges turn under properly at bamboo ring (fig. 64-H).

15. Repeat steps 11–14 for second bamboo ring, backing, and lining.

Christmas Scene

Here's Kris Kringle — all finished preparing his toys and goodies, and ready to share in the Yuletide festivities. One, two, or all three of these enchanting stockings, filled with treasures, can begin a new holiday tradition in your home; or make them as a very special gift.

Red and green bands of kalem stitch make the stockings look like old-fashioned leggings. You'll want this trio ready to hang on Christmas Eve, so take care to start early.

Design: Joanne and Robert Herzog.

1. Enlarge designs according to directions on page 12.

2. Bind edges of 21 by 36-inch piece of #7 (rug-type) canvas with masking tape. Draw outline of canvas on brown paper and mark as shown on page 13.

3. Roughly sketch stockings onto canvas with gray indelible marker.

4. Working from graph, stitch basketweave areas first, using 6 strands (1 full thread, doubled) of Persian yarn in a #16 tapestry needle. Begin stitching at the top and continue to the bottom, or vice versa.

5. Work bands of red and green in kalem stitch (page 25)

YARN COUNT

White
168½ yards

Light gray
18½ yards

Medium gray
3½ yards

Light wheat
13 yards

Wheat
5½ yards

Light fawn
7½ yards

Fawn
9 yards

Dark brown
16½ yards

Ice blue
36½ yards

Sky blue
25½ yards

Bright blue
1 yard

Pale yellow
13 yards

Golden yellow
3½ yards

Pale pink
1 yard

Dark pink
1 yard

STITCH GUIDE

Basketweave
Kalem (p. 25)

CANVAS

#7 rug-type
21 by 36-inch piece

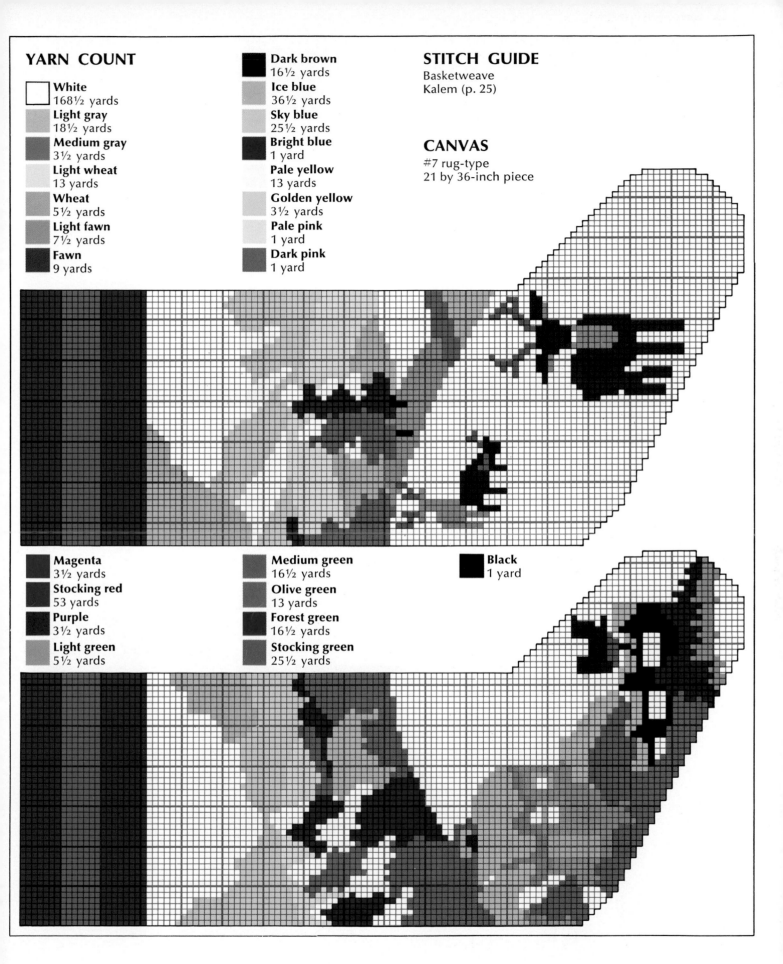

Magenta
3½ yards

Stocking red
53 yards

Purple
3½ yards

Light green
5½ yards

Medium green
16½ yards

Olive green
13 yards

Forest green
16½ yards

Stocking green
25½ yards

Black
1 yard

last, using 6 strands of Persian yarn.

6. Block according to directions on page 29.

FINISHING TECHNIQUES

You'll need: 2¼ yards of 36-inch-wide red velveteen, woven cotton, or polyester for backing, welting, and lining; 12 feet of ¼-inch-diameter cord for welting; three 7-inch lengths of twisted cord trim for loops (see page 31); sewing thread and needle.

Stockings

1. After blocking, machine stitch 2 rows through canvas around edges of needlepointed areas to prevent canvas threads from raveling; remove binding and trim excess canvas to 1 inch all around.

2. Use pattern saved from enlarged drawing, tracing it on lining and backing fabric; add 1-inch seam allowance all around. Cut 6 lining pieces and 3 backing pieces (fig. 68-A).

3. For each stocking, sew 2 lining pieces right sides together; leave top open.

4. Trim seams to ¼ inch all around.

5. Make welting according to directions on page 30.

6. Sew welting to needlepoint, finishing ends as shown on page 30.

7. Pin needlepoint to backing, right sides together, catching a twisted cord loop in back seam between the 2 thicknesses (fig. 68-B).

8. Stitch through needlepoint, welting, and backing, leaving top open. Clip curves for ease.

9. Turn stocking right side out; insert lining.

10. Turn under all raw edges along upper edge and blindstitch by hand (see fig. 68-C).

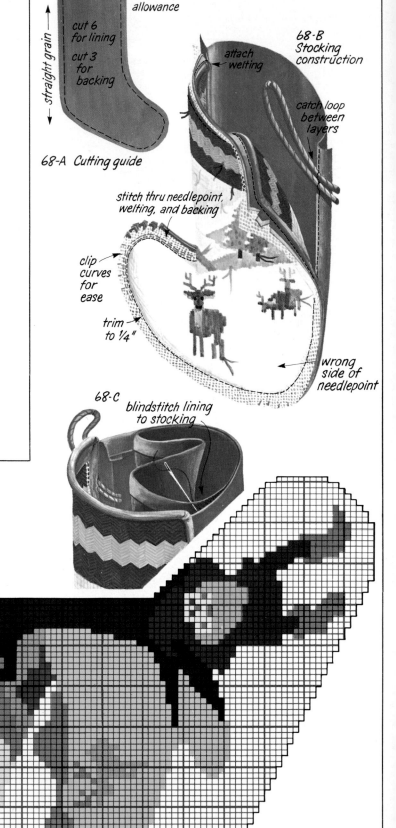

68-A Cutting guide

68-B Stocking construction

68-C blindstitch lining to stocking

Angel Baby

Delicate as the whispering wind, our little angel is sure to captivate all who see her. She is both a pillow and a soft, cuddly doll, worked in a variety of decorative stitches in two separate pieces — front and back. This needle-pointed charmer is fragile only in appearance, though, and will last to be treasured for years.

Bullion-stitched curls tumble about her rosy pink face, while Scotch stitches and French knots add subtle texture to her dress. Wings of warm, sunshine yellows are worked in long and short embroidery stitches, framing our angel in a halo of light.

Design: Jan Magdaleno.

1. Enlarge design according to directions on page 12.
2. Bind edges of two 16 by 18-inch pieces of #12 mono canvas for front and back; draw outline of canvas on brown paper and mark as shown on page 13.
3. Trace design onto canvas with gray indelible marker.
4. Stitch spots on hemline in basketweave, using 1 full thread of perle cotton in a #20 tapestry needle.
5. Stitch face, arms, bow, feet, and edge of dress (black outlines separate them from different stitches) in basket-weave, using 2 strands from a thread of Persian yarn.

6. Work dress in checkerboard Scotch stitch (see page 23) with 2 strands of Persian yarn.
7. Work dark blue areas in double leviathan stitch (see page 21), using 3 strands of Persian yarn.
8. Stitch French knots (see fig. 69-A) in centers of double leviathan stitches, using single strands of Persian yarn.
9. Work wings in long and short embroidery-type stitches (see fig. 70-A) with 3 strands of Persian yarn.
10. Stitch hair in bullion stitch (see fig. 70-B) with 3 strands of Persian yarn.
11. Block according to directions on page 29.

FINISHING TECHNIQUES

You'll need: ½ yard of 36-inch-wide muslin for inner pillow; polyester batting for stuffing; clear nylon thread and sewing needle.

After blocking, machine stitch 2 rows through canvas around needlepointed area to prevent canvas threads from raveling. Follow instructions on page 42 for making a knife-edge pillow; omit welting and use the 2 stitched pieces — no extra fabric is required.

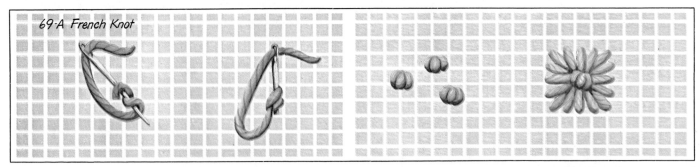

69-A French Knot

(Continued on next page)

ANGEL BABY PILLOW—FRONT

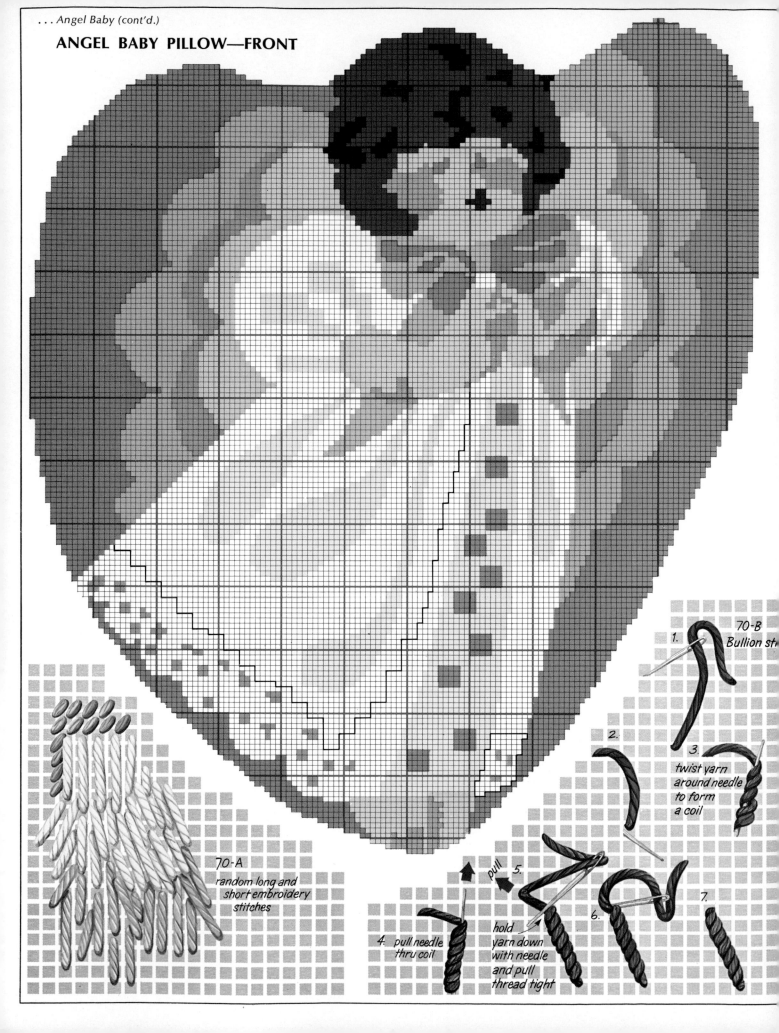

70-A
random long and
short embroidery
stitches

70-B
Bullion st

1.

2.

3. twist yarn
around needle
to form
a coil

4. pull needle
thru coil

pull

5.

hold
yarn down
with needle
and pull
thread tight

6.

7.

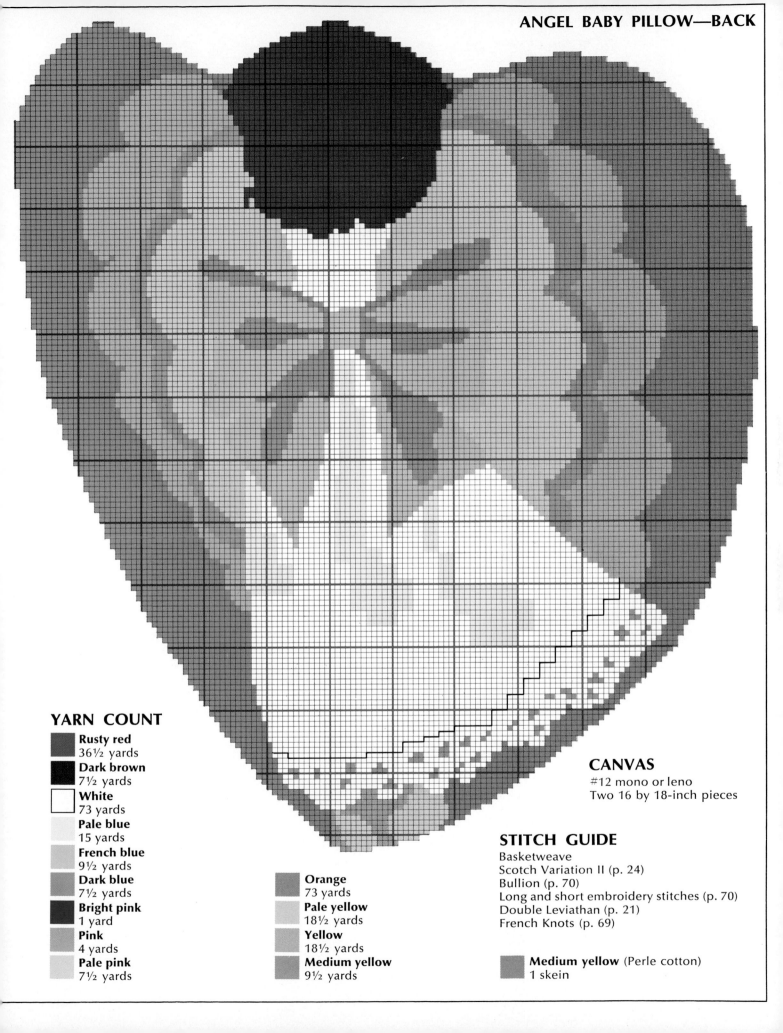

YARN COUNT

Rusty red
36½ yards

Dark brown
7½ yards

White
73 yards

Pale blue
15 yards

French blue
9½ yards

Dark blue
7½ yards

Bright pink
1 yard

Pink
4 yards

Pale pink
7½ yards

Orange
73 yards

Pale yellow
18½ yards

Yellow
18½ yards

Medium yellow
9½ yards

CANVAS

#12 mono or leno
Two 16 by 18-inch pieces

STITCH GUIDE

Basketweave
Scotch Variation II (p. 24)
Bullion (p. 70)
Long and short embroidery stitches (p. 70)
Double Leviathan (p. 21)
French Knots (p. 69)

Medium yellow (Perle cotton)
1 skein

Strawberry Basket

CANVAS
#10 mono or leno
19, 7, and 5-inch squares
6 by 55-inch band

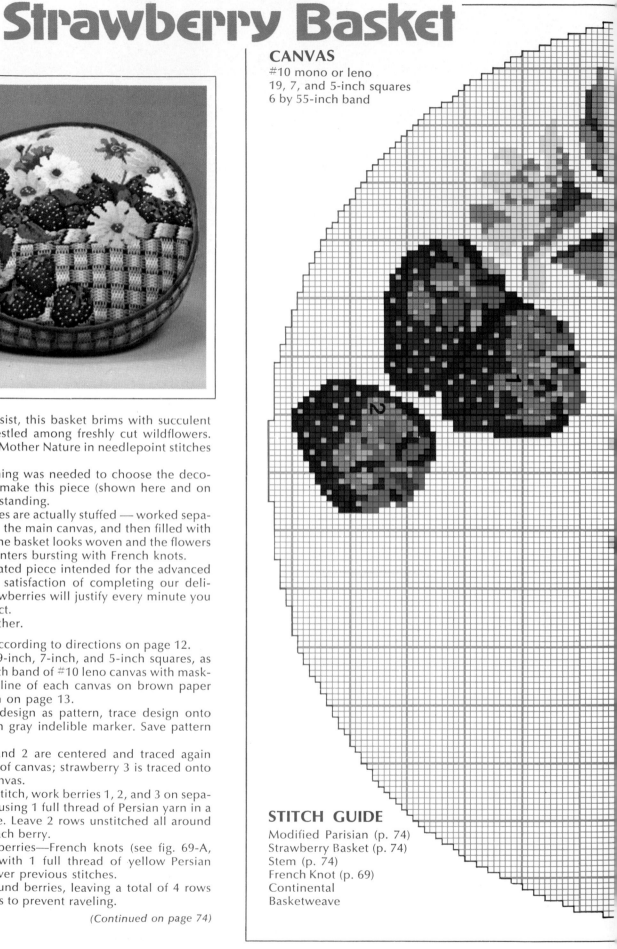

Too tempting to resist, this basket brims with succulent red strawberries nestled among freshly cut wildflowers. It elegantly mimics Mother Nature in needlepoint stitches of Persian yarn.

Thoughtful planning was needed to choose the decorative stitches that make this piece (shown here and on the front cover) outstanding.

Some of the berries are actually stuffed — worked separately, appliquéd to the main canvas, and then filled with polyester batting. The basket looks woven and the flowers seem alive, their centers bursting with French knots.

This is a complicated piece intended for the advanced needleworker. The satisfaction of completing our delicious basket of strawberries will justify every minute you devote to the project.

Design: Sue Walther.

1. Enlarge design according to directions on page 12.
2. Bind edges of 19-inch, 7-inch, and 5-inch squares, as well as a 6 by 55-inch band of #10 leno canvas with masking tape. Draw outline of each canvas on brown paper and mark as shown on page 13.
3. Using enlarged design as pattern, trace design onto 19-inch canvas with gray indelible marker. Save pattern for use in finishing.
4. Strawberries 1 and 2 are centered and traced again onto 7-inch square of canvas; strawberry 3 is traced onto 5-inch square of canvas.
5. In basketweave stitch, work berries 1, 2, and 3 on separate canvas pieces, using 1 full thread of Persian yarn in a #18 tapestry needle. Leave 2 rows unstitched all around within outline of each berry.
6. Work seeds of berries—French knots (see fig. 69-A, page 69) stitched with 1 full thread of yellow Persian yarn and worked over previous stitches.
7. Trim canvas around berries, leaving a total of 4 rows of unstitched canvas to prevent raveling.

(Continued on page 74)

STITCH GUIDE
Modified Parisian (p. 74)
Strawberry Basket (p. 74)
Stem (p. 74)
French Knot (p. 69)
Continental
Basketweave

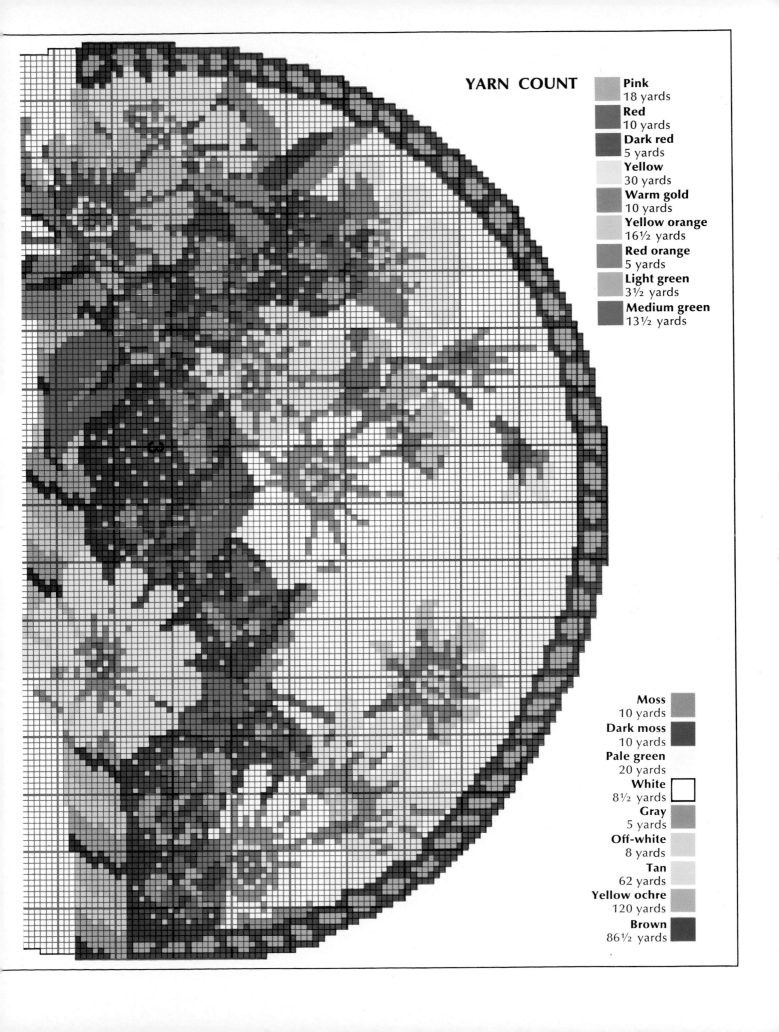

YARN COUNT

Pink
18 yards

Red
10 yards

Dark red
5 yards

Yellow
30 yards

Warm gold
10 yards

Yellow orange
16½ yards

Red orange
5 yards

Light green
3½ yards

Medium green
13½ yards

Moss
10 yards

Dark moss
10 yards

Pale green
20 yards

White
8½ yards

Gray
5 yards

Off-white
8 yards

Tan
62 yards

Yellow ochre
120 yards

Brown
86½ yards

8. Position berries on pillow front, matching grain of canvas, holes, and threads; pin to hold in place.

9. Using 1 full thread of Persian yarn in color indicated on graph, work continental stitch to appliqué berries to canvas, pulling yarn tight to avoid ridges. *Do not* leave opening for stuffing (see fig. 74-A).

10. Following graph, begin stitching main canvas by working centers of flowers in French knots (see fig. 69-A, page 69), using 2 strands from a thread of Persian yarn.

11. Stitch light green background in slightly varied Parisian stitch (see fig. 74-C). From this point on, project is worked with 1 full thread of Persian yarn.

12. Work basket and band in special stitch as shown in fig. 74-D using tan, yellow, ochre, and brown. Stitched area of band is 3 by 49 inches.

13. Stitch flowers, remaining strawberries, and leaves in basketweave or continental.

14. Work stems in stem stitch (see fig. 74-E).

15. Block both pillow front and band according to directions on page 29.

16. To stuff appliquéd berries, turn canvas to wrong side and cut 1-inch slit widthwise into bare canvas behind berries 1, 2, and 3. Be sure to leave at least 3 uncut canvas threads between stitching and slit. Stuff berries very full with polyester batting. Whipstitch separate piece of canvas over each slit with strong white thread (see fig. 74-B).

FINISHING TECHNIQUES

You'll need: 1 yard of 36-inch-wide velveteen for backing and welting; matching thread; 110 inches of ¼-inch-diameter cord for welting; ¾ yard of 36-inch-wide muslin for inner pillow; polyester batting for stuffing; clear nylon thread and sewing needle.

Pillow Cover

1. Machine stitch 2 rows through canvas around entire needlepointed area to prevent canvas threads from raveling; remove binding and trim excess canvas to 1 inch all around.

2. Finish as for pincushion on page 36, using stitched band as boxing. Use enlarged drawing as pattern to cut backing and inner pillow covering.

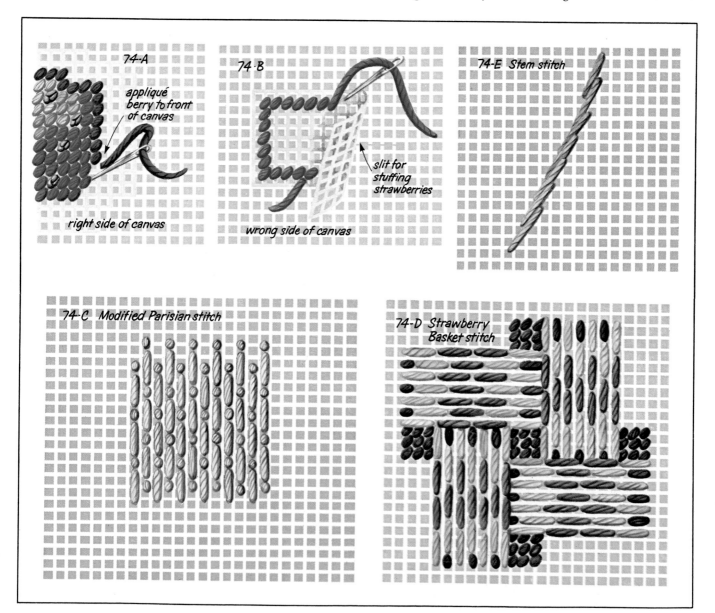

74-A appliqué berry to front of canvas / right side of canvas

74-B slit for stuffing strawberries / wrong side of canvas

74-E Stem stitch

74-C Modified Parisian stitch

74-D Strawberry Basket stitch

Pussy Willow Tote

Fresh and delicate as the first hint of spring is the design of silky catkins and a petit point butterfly on this cylindrical tote. The 15 by 18-inch finished needlepoint would make a lovely pillow, too.

Design: Marinda Brown.

1. Enlarge design according to directions on page 12.
2. Bind edges of a 19 by 22-inch piece of 10/20 penelope canvas with masking tape. Draw outline of canvas on brown paper and mark as shown on page 13.
3. Trace design onto canvas with gray indelible marker.
4. Using graph below left, stitch butterfly in petit point (either basketweave or continental) with 6 strands of embroidery floss in a #20 tapestry needle (see page 6). White squares are French knots (see fig. 69-A, page 69).
5. In basketweave or continental, work pussy willows and background using 2 strands from a thread of Persian yarn.
6. Block according to directions on page 29.

FINISHING TECHNIQUES

You'll need: 19 by 25-inch piece of canvas or linen for lining; ½ yard imitation suede fabric (see fig. 75-A); matching thread; clear nylon thread and sewing needle; two 1½-inch-diameter brass rings; one 16-inch zipper; 62 inches of ¼-inch-diameter cord for welting; 1 flag halyard snap (see fig. 76-D).

Pussy Willow Tote

1. After blocking, machine stitch 2 rows through canvas around edges of needlepointed areas to prevent canvas threads from raveling; remove binding and trim excess canvas to 1 inch all around.
2. Fold canvas in half widthwise and mark a dot at center point of each side.
3. Cut out fabric pieces as shown in figure 75-A, at right,

DETAIL—BUTTERFLY

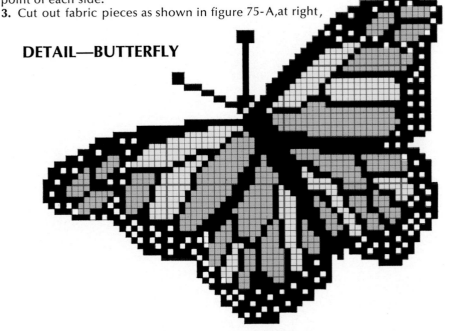

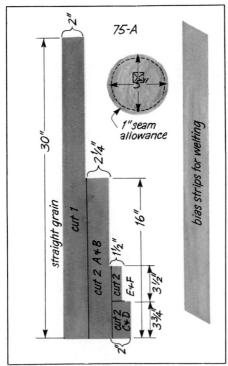

75-A

and mark on wrong side of fabric.

4. Make two 31-inch lengths of welting (see page 30).

5. Stitch zipper to parts A and B; see package directions.

6. Using ½-inch seam allowances, stitch parts C and D to zippered section, and topstitch seams (see fig. 76-A). You now have a rectangle measuring 3¾ by 18 inches.

7. Stitch top edge of needlepoint to one 18-inch side of zippered rectangle, right sides together; stitch bottom edge to other side of rectangle, forming a cylinder open at both ends (see fig. 76-B).

8. Turn bag right side out and stitch a length of welting to each end of cylinder, joining ends of welting as shown on page 30. Start and end welting at dot (fig. 76-B).

9. To make end tabs E and F that hold brass rings, fold along fold lines, wrong sides together, and topstitch ⅛ inch from edge (see fig. 76-C).

10. Fold ends back as shown, catching brass ring in fold. Stitch to 1 end circle of tote where marked (see fig. 76-D).

11. Repeat steps 9 and 10 for other side of bag and ring.

12. With wrong sides out, stitch circles to body of bag, matching dots; use zipper foot to stitch near welting.

13. Turn edges in and handstitch lining to bag; then turn bag right side out.

14. Fold edges of strap in ½ inch, wrong sides together, and topstitch ¼ inch from edge.

15. Attach one end of strap to first brass ring, turning raw edge under. Attach halyard snap to other end in same manner and hook to second brass ring (see fig. 76-D).

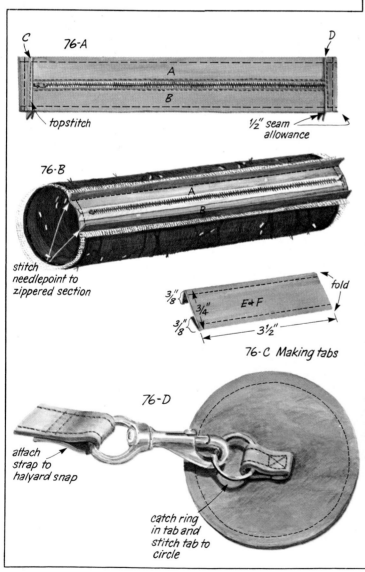

76-A

topstitch ½" seam allowance

76-B

stitch needlepoint to zippered section

⅜" ¾" E+F fold
⅜" 3½"

76-C Making tabs

76-D

attach strap to halyard snap

catch ring in tab and stitch tab to circle

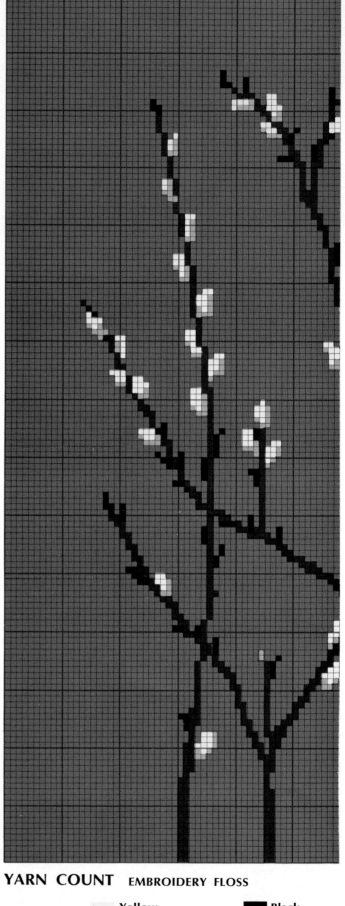

YARN COUNT EMBROIDERY FLOSS

	Yellow 1 skein		**Black** 1 skein
	Warm orange 1 skein		**White** 1 skein

PUSSY WILLOW TOTE

PERSIAN

■ **Brown**
18 yards

■ **Black**
9 yards

□ **Pale gray**
9 yards

▨ **Gray**
9 yards

■ **Malt brown**
171 yards

STITCH GUIDE Basketweave (petit point and gros point)

CANVAS 10/20 penelope
19 by 22-inch piece

Bargello Typewriter Cover

A bland gray plastic typewriter cover is happily replaced by the handsomely stitched bargello cover pictured above.

Since typewriters vary greatly in size and shape, our directions will serve only as a basic guide for making a cover to fit your own machine. This cover design can be adapted to any typewriter shape or size, once the basic line of the bargello pattern is established.

As a pattern, use the plastic cover that came with your typewriter. Center and trace the cover outline onto a 30 by 36-inch piece of #13 bargello canvas with an indelible marker.

If your typewriter doesn't have a plastic cover, make a pattern for your bargello cover by taking measurements as shown in figure 79-A; then roughly sketch this outline onto your canvas.

Design: Diane L. Dyson.

1. With masking tape, bind edges of a piece of #13 bargello canvas cut sufficiently large to allow an extra 3 inches all around cover design.
2. After drawing outline as described, fold canvas lengthwise to find vertical center; mark center bottom with pencil.
3. Following graph, stitch 1 complete row of bargello pattern from center bottom out to sides of outline.
4. Continue stitching from bottom to top, following basic

pattern as established in step 3. Roll canvas and secure with safety pins as you work, to keep stitched area out of your way.
5. Steam press piece on wrong side, pulling slightly as you go to ease it into shape; bargello work does not require blocking.

FINISHING TECHNIQUES

You'll need: Fabric for sides and welting, such as velveteen; matching thread; lightweight cotton or polyester fabric for lining (optional); ¼-inch-diameter cord for welting; sewing thread and needle. (Note: When you shop for finishing fabric, take needlepoint and pattern pieces with you.)

Typewriter Cover

1. After pressing, machine stitch 2 rows through canvas around edges of needlepointed area to prevent canvas threads from raveling; remove binding and trim excess canvas to 1 inch all around. Cut pattern for lining.
2. Make pattern for sides (see fig. 79-A). Cut 2 pieces at once from fabric folded with right sides together.
3. Make enough welting to fit upper curved edge of *each*

side piece and to outline entire base perimeter of finished cover.

4. Right sides together, using a zipper foot, sew welting to curved edge *only* of each side piece, stitching close to welting and leaving ¼ inch of welting extending down past *both* ends of straight bottom edge of each side piece.

5. Right sides facing, pin side pieces to main body of cover along welting seam; stitch, using zipper foot. Clip curves for ease; trim seams to ¼ inch; turn right side out.

6. Align edge of welting seam allowance with lower edge of typewriter cover, right sides facing; pin into place

and stitch with zipper foot, joining welting ends as shown on page 30. Turn welting seam allowance to inside of cover and blindstitch to hold.

7. If you choose to line cover, cut sides and body, using patterns cut in steps 1 and 2.

8. Join sides and body of lining as for cover, omitting welting. Clip curves and press seam open. *Do not* turn right side out.

9. Pin lining to inside of cover; turn raw edges under and blindstitch (see page 39, fig. 39-F) to cover. Tack along side seams to hold lining in place.

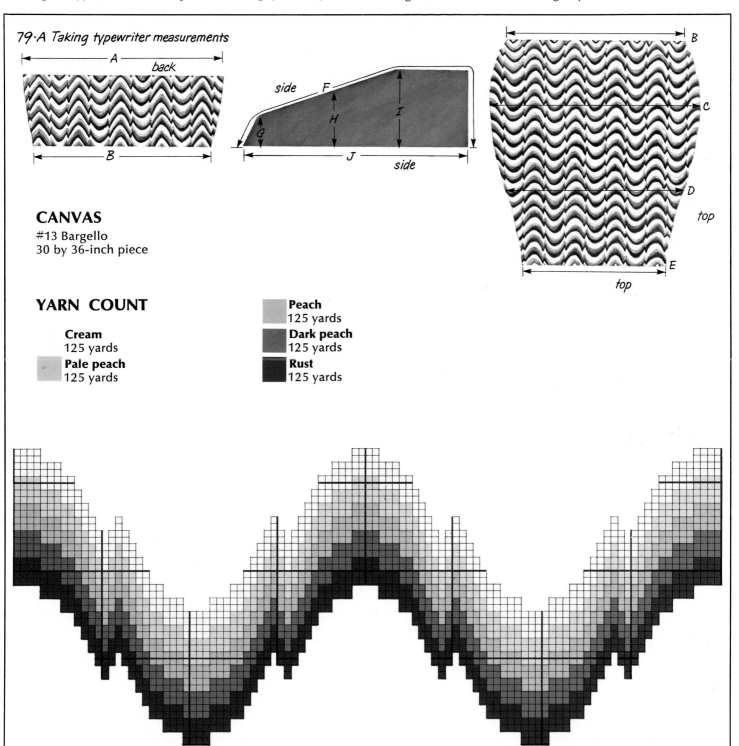

79-A Taking typewriter measurements

CANVAS
#13 Bargello
30 by 36-inch piece

YARN COUNT

Cream
125 yards

Pale peach
125 yards

Peach
125 yards

Dark peach
125 yards

Rust
125 yards

Index